The Lion's Mouth

KATHLEEN RAINE

The Lion's Mouth

*Concluding Chapters
of Autobiography*

And last, the rending pain of re-enactment
  Of all that you have done, and been; the shame
  Of motives late revealed, and the awareness
Of things ill done and done to others' harm
  Which once you took for exercise of virtue.

T. S. ELIOT, *Little Gidding*

HAMISH HAMILTON
LONDON

First published in Great Britain 1977
by Hamish Hamilton Ltd
90 Great Russell Street London WC1B 3PT

Copyright © 1977 by Kathleen Raine

SBN 241 89756 4

The quotation from "Little Gidding"
which appears on the title-page is published
by kind permission of Mrs. T. S. Eliot
and Messrs. Faber and Faber

Printed in Great Britain by
Western Printing Services Ltd, Bristol

INTRODUCTION

THIS is the third and final section of a record I wrote in 1962 at a time when the writing of my story seemed to me the only way in which, by seeking to understand my life, I could go on living it. In this perhaps vain attempt I hoped to come to some understanding of life itself, its meaning and its purpose; and whose life can we know if not our own? To each of us a life is entrusted for whose years and days we are ourselves responsible, once it is ours, from whatever deeper roots it may have sprung. The earlier sections of my story, although I wrote it as a whole and wish it might have been read, if at all, as a whole, have already been published. Those who might have been hurt by anything written in those earlier chapters—above all my father and my mother—are no longer living. The only person to whom this last part of my story can now do injury is myself.

In 1966 I wrote what I then thought was a concluding section; but Gavin's death in 1971 showed that ending also not to have been the end. Now nothing more can, in this life, ever be added.

In revising the first version and the second I have not changed what I originally wrote. This has made of the manuscript a kind of palimpsest, in which the later additions will, I hope, be clearly seen as such.

I would be glad to think that my life has been worse than those of most of my fellow-beings who may read this book. But let those who blame me consider that, as Dante found in Hell, we walk at all times a perilous knife-edge between good and evil, and there is no mistake or misdeed so blind or so fatal that we ourselves might not have made it. But

1

neither is there any so lost as to be unaware of the good that might have been, who does not mourn that loss continually in a heart however frozen. I think that Dante understood, in meeting the souls of the damned and of the blessed and of those toiling their way, like most of us, through our purgatory, that each has its story which, stripped of the outer personality and its pretences, must be told; understood that every soul not only has, but is, its own truth. The damned are from their own mouths condemned, even in their self-justification; and the beatitude of the blessed is in the very fact of their joy. Yet experience, however terrible, cannot fail to purchase a little wisdom, 'at the price of all that a man hath', as Blake says, 'in the desolate market where none comes to buy'.

Morally speaking perhaps I ought to despair, yet I do not, nor would I wish to lead others to commit that deadliest of all sins. A lifetime is perhaps only an episode in the soul's long history. Perhaps each soul is an unique being, living many lives in its long pilgrimage towards the distant goal of which the wise have told us. Or it may be that we discover, by degrees, that our seeming identities are in reality only aspects or parts of a whole infinitely greater than ourselves, episodes in the one life of humanity; or it may be that our lives are, in Blake's words, only 'deadly dreams the soul falls into when it leaves Eden, following the Serpent'.

I put the decision whether to publish or not to publish in the hands of friends. First, Valerie Eliot, who has urged me to tell my story; I can only think because she is one of those women whose concern is with love, and who has herself truly loved. Her lot in love has been in all ways opposite to mine, for she made happy the man she loved. That happy marriage, so late in her great poet's life that it might have seemed a possibility no longer even to be hoped for, has become a crown of his work, something added to the poetry that T. S. Eliot's life itself has bequeathed to us; a vindication of all that had led up to that happy and harmonious conclusion after so much suffering on the way. The poetry

2

itself has received from his late and happy marriage a kind of validation; for the love of poets is so high a vision that it condemns many to loneliness and disappointed hopes which in their turn call such love itself in question. How very wonderful it is—how rare—to know that such a poet as Eliot found love's realisation not impossible.

Second, Philip Sherrard, a friend and intellectual companion with whom for thirty years I have been in the habit of conversing on the living issues of the soul which I would call philosophy had not that word become meaningless in common parlance. The third to read this story is Rafael Nadal, once the poet Lorca's friend, and for many years mine; a man of that great Western European culture whose values are shared by all whom I have ever called friends. At first I had hesitated to let him see this record, fearing that his Spanish courtesy would restrain him from speaking all his mind; but I should have known that in matters of what is written, and still more what is published there could be for him only one rule, Plotinus' "There is nothing higher than the truth." The fourth is Antonia White. She it was whose influence chiefly led me to become a Catholic convert. I have since wavered and vacillated, finally (insofar as anything is final) unable to remain within the framework of the Church to which she has remained faithful. Her steadfastness I honour; as I do those standards by which she measures all human conduct, those of the great Catholic Christian tradition. There is no better conscience in any human being than that tradition, and I am content to be judged by Antonia by that measure of perfection which offers to sinners like myself not any permissive condoning of what we have done but the possibility of the forgiveness of our sins. The Church knows, from its two thousand years of experience, that we are all sinners and that aspiring to perfection we but fall into spiritual pride.

To these friends therefore I have submitted my story; not in the hope that they may find excuses for me, but because I care only for the judgement of men who are wise, and of

3

women who have loved. Not all clever men are wise, not all women experienced in sex know love; which is also wisdom, as wisdom must be of the nature of love. With judgements made in terms of lesser values I have no concern. These four I thank for criticisms and suggestions, some, but not all of which, I have followed. Their verdict is that, on balance, I should publish; but the final responsibility can only be my own. And I must add the name of yet one more friend, Rita Langford, who has typed this manuscript for me.

February 9th, 1977.   KATHLEEN RAINE

The Tree and its Fruit

Io ho tenutoi piedi in quella parte della vita, di là dalla quale non
si puo ire per intendento di ritornare.

Dante: *La vita nuova.*

TOO MUCH happens to us in the present world for it to
be possible to preserve a sure sense of what is really
ours. We think we 'know' what we possess merely by
hearsay, or from books, or on the word of other people.
Our lives are encumbered with irrelevancies which we
mistake for living experience, and which in the end come
more and more to usurp it. Perhaps we cannot bring ourselves to admit what has at other times been clearly understood, that one life cannot encompass every possibility but
can realize only one.

What we have lived for may prove to be some few occasions, perhaps some single event, in which we have known
ourselves to be agents of, and participators in, a life greater
than our own. Our deepest realizations, whether of knowledge or of love, are not our own inventions or discoveries
or plans, but come, as it seems, by revelation. Edwin Muir
when he wrote of 'the story' and 'the fable' understood this
very well. Our story is too often—as mine has been—the
record of our failure to embody in our lives the enduring
pattern of 'the fable'. But then—and Edwin said this also—
how can we, knowing so little of that lost record of what
should have been, struggling as we are in the dark, hope to
do better? And yet is it not precisely from the dark that we
are guided? When for a moment we succeed in silencing the
endless prattle of the conscious mind and listen, do we not
become aware of presences, watching us with rapt attention,

5

'full of eyes', as the Bible says of spiritual intelligences? What if of those beings—and may they not be our true selves—we are but the instruments? For what purposes how can we know? For to the daimons our lives are not means to such ends as we might wish. Their ends may indeed bring us to greater happiness than we could have dreamed; but equally —perhaps also—those purposes may destroy the mortal actors, their instruments, in the process, for love and death have always been their favourite play. Those natural friends who are, according to Blake, 'spiritual enemies', would always save us if they could from the gods; who have, besides, as Odysseus complained to Athene, a way of absenting themselves at crucial moments, leaving us to our own devices. Very rightly, for the task of life, once assigned, is, after all, our own.

St. Teresa said to her divine lover that it is not surprising He has so few friends, He treats them so badly. 'It is a terrible thing to fall into the hands of the living God.' All have found it so. Yet it is said that none is given a task beyond his strength. If we fail we have no right to complain that what was required of us was too difficult. What is asked, is, always, precisely what is appropriate: it is our own fate and no other that comes to us in our appointed time. For in reality fate is itself a kind of choice; made not consciously but with the whole of our being, which responds only to that to which it is attuned. And of all things the worst is to fail, not in those relationships and activities which were never really ours, but in that inner and predestined calling to which each of us is born. A vocation, surely, always of love, for what is love unless that deep attraction to what is our own?

What brought me to my appointed task was no act of my own will but of those others who for a while unveiled their world and assigned me my part. During the enacting of this, the central event in my life, I seemed to follow the form of an unfolding myth and to embody a meaning which as I lived it I both knew and did not know.

In describing, then, the fate that came, in its appointed

time, to me (as it comes to all) I wish neither to expose nor to conceal anything, because mine. I have no right to call 'mine' one more story among the infinite number of stories woven by ever-various life. I wish only to bear witness, for the greater glory of the mystery whose curtain was withdrawn for a moment, so tenuously glimpsed and quickly lost. For I, who had for long periods lived my life in places which were not my place, and among people who were not my people, did come at last to what was my own. There must be some who have never known this happiness; for even if what is ours be some deep suffering or death itself, to miss what is ours is to miss all.

The external events have perhaps little to do with my story; this being the record of an inner experience as it reflected itself in the outer world; as if, for a time, that world itself were a living region of consciousness, like the landscape of dream. The other person who shared these events would have had another story to tell; did in fact tell another story. Yet at the time I thought our two lives part of a single whole greater than either. Was I then blinded to objective truth by self-delusion? Or am I, in now doubting the truth of my own experience, blinded by outer events to the inner and abiding reality?

*

Eden is rather a state than a place; yet it is a state that makes its own those places in which we have experienced the state. As a child at Bavington* I had experienced that happiness of finding in all about me the reflected radiance of what I then still was—myself. At Martindale** I had entered it again, as it seems, through the magic of natural love. Now for a third time I was to be allowed to return from exile; and again through love, though in a different mode, as if, at each return, some deeper insight had been given into a reality in itself ever the same.

---

* See *Farewell, Happy Fields*   ** See *The Land Unknown*

It seems strange, now I consider it, that in all the years I had lived at Martindale, and even later, when I had stayed so often with Helen Sutherland at Cockley Moor, that I had never once thought of the possibility of going back to Bavington. Doubtless I was right—the distance of Bavington was not a distance of mere miles, but of years, or of something more than years. And yet people do revisit the places they have loved, and such returns have in themselves meaning. Doubtless for me the time had not yet come. I had become another person from that country child who had carried water from the village well and run barefoot about the high pastures. In part I had disinherited myself through estrangement from my family. 'Honour thy father and thy mother that thy days may be long in the land that the Lord thy God giveth thee'; these words had hung above my bed in the blue bedroom of the Manse; and with these words I had broken faith. I seldom saw Aunt Peggy herself, now; living in retirement, in the south of England, with my mother's sister Jean. I had moved into another world from theirs; fulfilling too well my parents' ambition for me. In becoming 'educated' I had moved away from those simple things I had loved as a child. But then, they too had moved away, into the world of suburbia and its mass-produced trash, bargain sales in Oxford Street, into new convenient houses furnished from the cheaper department stores, discarding all that at Bavington had seemed so permanent and beautiful. The ground we had shared in common was, but for memory, no longer there. Not only education, but an entire reorientation of my life by ideas and experiences, by music, painting and poetry, by friendships, by a whole range of immeasurable values, had removed me from the simple society of my early Eden.

There were practical reasons too, of course, why I had not returned. I simply had not had the money for the journey, for one thing. There was the war, and people tended not to travel at that time. My children were young, and from Martindale, or from Cockley Moor, Penrith, our market town, seemed at the extreme of traversable distance. Psychologically this was so; and how much there is to be said for those contained worlds in which we at different times ensphere ourselves, lest we become dissolved in a landscape too ever-shifting to gather meaning. But it had been some more positive force which had kept me away, some sense that the gates were closed, that I was forbidden. That child I had been and the world she had inhabited had become for me mere regions of memory; I had not dared to admit to myself how wide the distances that now divided me from my old identity; from my true identity and the only place I had ever felt to be my real home. For me the Manse was still there, as it had been; I knew that to return to Bavington would be to discover that I could not return. Perhaps it was also a sense of guilt for all I had since done and become, or that had befallen me, that kept me away.

But at some time after the war—although the war had nothing to do with that change of inner disposition—I began to hope that I was on the way of return; that all was not lost, or that the lost might still be found again. I could but return as a stranger. Yet now it seemed to me as if, by visiting again those places, a rift might be healed, and I might recover something of that former self and state of being. With astonishment I realized how near, in mere physical distance, those Northumbrian moors were to Martindale, to Cockley Moor, to Lanercost (at the other end of Hadrian's Wall I had once known so well) where Winifred Nicholson lived in her father's house.

Long before I came to know her at Cockley Moor (where many of her paintings hung) I had known Winifred's north-country flowers against north-country skies of luminous grey cloud. How, I had wondered, could she have come to see flowers in that indescribable, especial way that I had known them as a child? Wild flowers I had not seen for years, and country garden-flowers, painted in that especial light—I did not so put it to myself then, but that light is the light of Paradise. I did not see the world as Ben Nicholson saw it;

9

nor—although at Ben's suggestion she illustrated my first book of poems—as Barbara Hepworth saw it. My Cambridge-trained intellect, indeed, understood Barbara's hard crystals and solid geometry. Nor did I quite see nature aflame in the sacramental Christian vision as David Jones saw his Roland's Tree or his Welsh Madonna encircled with native thorns and native roses. A greater painter than Winifred, doubtless; but my simple affinity of seeing was with her.

I was first introduced to her by Henry Moore, at an exhibition in which both had works; and thought her face as lovely as her paintings. When at Cockley Moor I met her again we became friends; and the beginning of my story—for this story has a beginning, a middle, and an end—was a visit to Winifred, then living at her father's manor-house, Boothby near Lanercost.

It was from Boothby that one August day with my two children (they older now than I had been as that former child), I set out to bicycle along the Roman wall. I remember that Winifred had talked to me of Goethe's theory of colour, about which she had been reading in some Anthroposophical book; and I remember how the subtle mauve of the Crane's-bill by the roadside was luminous on that day of our setting out to bicycle from the Banks to Wark; how the yellow of dandelion and mimulus seemed to pour towards us; how the perfect blue of the sky opened great distances. With enhanced senses I was re-entering the landscapes so long ago loved. All seemed to conspire to enhance and brighten that late summer scene into which we that day set forth.

The North Tyne at Wark was just as I had remembered that broad, shallow salmon-river moving with rippling grace over its stones; my grandfather's river, whence he had drawn those flower-fragrant little trout and shining salmon that were for me a memory even earlier than the Manse. But the distance from Wark to Bavington seemed to have shrunk to a few inconspicuous miles. The Manse, though now its trees were felled and its garden ruined and rank was, to my surprise, not smaller than I had remembered; though I did not enter the house. The Lady's Mantle still grew by the kirk wall, the sweet scent of camomile and cow-dung in the farmyard was just as it had been, and the cold, pure water still stirred the sand-grains in the stone well where I had filled my buckets all those years ago. Granny Carr's scarlet tropaeolum still entwined the great yew-tree in her garden; and her son George, as old now as she had been then, still grew, in that fertile earth, sweet-peas, carnations and his own tobacco-crop, all of a luxuriance whose secret died with him. The line of Simonside with its triple summit lay still on the horizon, as once on the periphery of the world; but now I came from beyond the periphery and the centre had become strange. The school was closed now and had become a youth-hostel; and it was there that George Carr, to whom I had written asking him to find us rooms, had put us to sleep; he was now the warden, as formerly his mother had been the school caretaker.

Strange it was to sleep in that room, my children and I on narrow camp-beds, where I had learned to write and figure on a squeaky slate, with a row of friendly faces beside me, lulled by the chanting of multiplication tables. The lattice of roses painted on the wall by my Aunty Peggy's predecessor was still there, and the iron stove and the smell of carbolic soap still lingered in the lobby. It was, I do not know why, one of the worst nights I have ever passed; though what that nightmare was I have not remembered; only a certain atmosphere heavy and oppressive as the spirit of the grave.

Next day I learned that almost every farm I had known was now occupied by the children who had been my school-fellows; all intermarried now, Waltons and Robsons and Thorntons and Scotts. I took my children to Clay Walls, where the younger sister of my old friend Sally Walton was now married to a schoolfellow; and drying plates in the back-kitchen with her I felt a deep pang of nostalgia, realizing how much happier my own children might have been, had they been born into this or some other of those dignified

11

stone farm-houses that stand so high on the open hills. I had wished for no happier future than to become a farmer's wife, like my school-fellows; and with a pang I wondered if all my life had not been astray from those simple fields; but that had not, after all, been the land that God had given me.

Next day, in Wark, we supped with my old playfellow herself, now a farmer's wife, living in country abundance. She had remembered me: her daughter was called Kathleen. But when we left after that happy visit I felt ashamed that they had so welcomed me back. Their lives, I felt, had kept faith; and I was not even a prodigal, for I could never return. I felt myself an impostor, guilty of a deception, in pretending to be the Kathie they had known; as if I had been acting a part. Yet who was I? In imagination times and places and people abide for ever as they were; but the reality of this world is also inexorable.

*

It is hard to recover radical innocence, to be absolved of all we have become, to be as if we had never departed from the abiding ground and centre of the soul of which almost every act is a betrayal; but there are times when, despite all, it is as if lost Paradise might be the end, as it is the beginning, of our journey. For what I did not find at Bavington I found awaiting me on my return to London.

AE wrote of that lost ground of the soul, 'Just as your will joins your two hands together for one purpose, so the one consciousness which pierces up and down through every plane of being brings you and another together. It is well to know the meaning of the mystic hours as they pass.' For, as the two hands are joined, I was brought together with another person, caught up, as it seemed, in the same swirl and eddy of immortal life.

Within a few days of my return to Paulton's Square, Gavin came to my house for the first time. He was brought by Tambimuttu, who had, most characteristically, called some dozen or more times during my absence for the sole

12

purpose of arranging this meeting. I had no great wish to meet the kind of person likely to be brought by Tambi, but then one never knew. Tambi's friends could be (not metaphorically but literally) princes or beggars, distinguished poets or drug addicts. Under persuasion I allowed him to bring Gavin Maxwell who wanted, so Tambi said, to paint my portrait. The idea was entirely Tambi's as it transpired; Gavin, it seems, had lost all his money and was also just recovering from a breakdown; and Tambi was being kind to him, encouraging him to write poems and to take up the career of portrait painting, which at that time seemed his best hope of recovering his fortunes. The thing was, Tambi said, to have an exhibition with paintings of famous people in it, as a kind of bait for custom; and in the warmth of his loyalty Tambi thought of Kathleen, his 'great poet': Gavin should paint her. So Gavin, perhaps as uninterested as I was myself in the meeting, was brought to my door. I took very little notice of him, or he of me; perhaps he was wondering, as I had been of him, what could be wrong with me that I should be a friend of that prince of bohemians. Yet my acquaintance with Tambi was, so to say, legitimate, since I was a poet and he my first publisher; but who was Gavin and how came he to know Tambi? His paintings, when I saw them, were extremely conventional. Yet Tambi was right in discerning, in Gavin, a vein of genius. Tambi's gift was for recognizing people of genius; the work followed.

I can still recall Gavin's appearance on that day, and my own impression of him. He was like some blind bird (perhaps the hawk his own name names), its restless energy a torment to itself for want of sight. It was as if those lids that cover the eyes of nestlings covered the eyes of his spirit. Why Tambi had brought him to me I could not imagine; yet he persisted. He made Gavin set up a camera and take my photograph; then he drove us out into my garden where, under the pear-tree I had inherited from Cooie Lane who had loved it before me, he stood Gavin and myself together, like a reluctant Adam and Even, and photographed

13

us so. Yet I think both Gavin and myself had quite made up our minds that there it should end. I dislike being photographed or painted, not so much because I dislike my own appearance but because the idea that I am visible at all disturbs me. I do not like to be seen. But then, as Gavin was about to leave, I chanced to say that I had just returned from Northumberland. It then emerged that my places of imagination were his also. It was his grandfather, the Duke of Northumberland, who owned those salmon-waters whence my grandfather had drawn those shining fish; the fir-plantation at Kielder whence had come the pheasant who once had looked at me with jewelled eye; the hill, the heather, the wild thyme, the lichen on the stone, all were his. Gavin was native of my paradise.

Those amongst whom I had lived my adult life had all been strangers to my childhood. They took me for someone who had never been that child. I had been able to survive in exile because I had retained an inviolate sanctuary of imaginative solitude beyond the reach of Cambridge and its destructive cleverness. A part of me had remained, remote and unassailable, in my own country; and by virtue of that inviolate interior world I had been a poet. All my poems that are of any value had come from that solitude. I had believed not only that no other person did share, but that no other person could share, that thrice-encircled place. I had neither the wish nor the expectation of meeting any other living soul who could enter my sanctuary. Now another had crossed the magic threshold; had, it seemed, been there from the beginning. I had met by miracle another person who came from my first world; and because he came from the places where Eden had been, it was as if he came from Eden itself.

Dismissing Tambi with aristocratic adroitness he arranged to meet me the same evening. Then and later we mingled memories. He showed me photographs of the child he had been; and I showed one to him of my infant self standing on the little bridge at Kielder from which he too had looked down into the same swirling burn. All the treasured lore which to my mother's family had made his half legendary, I offered as balm for those wounds and humiliations which had brought him, by ways so devious, to my door. But above all it was in nature, in the wild world above the frontiers of the human, where he and I alike, released from whatever in the human world we were or seemed or were compelled to be, had found our escape and our joy. Both of us in childhood had inhabited that unfallen world; and there the Duke's grandchild and the schoolmaster's met as one. I found in him what I had found in no other person, a knowledge which had always been mine: not a scientist's knowledge of nature (though he was a naturalist of some distinction) but a knowledge by participation, the knowledge nature has of itself; for both of us nature had been, and still was, a region of consciousness. 'We two were born upon the self-same hill'; and there is something in the very light, the taste of wet wind, clouds, moors sweet with heather or white under snow, that in him and me alike had wedded our imaginations to a certain kind of place, and to no other; as curlews will nest only on moors, gull and guillemot on rocky ledges by the sea.

But if his grandfather was of Northumberland Gavin himself was of the country beyond the border, the legendary land of my mother's people: Scotland. The house of his other grandfather (the naturalist Sir Herbert Maxwell), was Monreith, in Wigtonshire; north of the Solway. Why, in the company of Englishmen, had I never felt at ease or among my own? Gavin belonged to my own people in the country lost before I was born. If it was in reality my mother who had secretly implanted in me her own nostalgia, her longing to return to her own country, God knows I experienced that longing as my own.

Was it that very day, or a few days later, that I was standing in my bedroom late at night before going to bed; and I could see, for that time, into two worlds, as if, waking, one were at the same time to explore a dream. But the quality

15

was different from that of all but a few dreams. As I had once held my breath to see the flow of immortal life in a hyacinth, so did I to see the Tree, though it stood in inner space, not in nature. May-tree or Rowan, it bore its clusters of white flowers. In it was a blackbird and at the foot the sleeping figure of a young boy of about twelve years old. The tree was on the summit of a hill, and I was aware of the flow of waters into its roots, gathered from the darkness and cold storms I knew to be raging below. The tree itself, the laden branches, the singing of the bird and the flow of life from chaos and cold to form and flower and fruit was all, I knew, taking place in the mind of the sleeper; all was his thought, his dream raising the tree and its flowers continually into being. I saw neither serpent nor wall round the garden; my tree stood wild and free, uncircumscribed and without any symbol of evil.

What do such visions mean? No explanation could ever 'mean' as much as the experience itself; for such visions are intellections, a mode of knowledge. It seemed an anamnesis of the soul's native place, the immortal world, the reality within and beyond appearances; the same that I had seen in the hyacinth. That is what it seemed to be; a reality glimpsed and lost again when normal consciousness closed in upon me. What I saw did not seem strange, but so deeply familiar that the outer world seems strange in comparison; something at once seen and understood, as a complex yet single thought; that, and the supernatural beauty; for nothing in that world is a mere thing, or object, but sacred; being life itself. I had been taken to the very place I had set out to find when with my children I had returned to Bavington, but had not found there.

Because these things had come to me unsought—the vision of the Tree, the meeting with Gavin like a messenger from home—I thought them Heaven-sent. It was as if the outer event, the meeting with Gavin, belonged to the same order of reality as the vision itself, outer and inner worlds miraculously coinciding. It seemed as if I had, unawares, discovered some lost secret and passed from the unreal into the real. Because Gavin had come from that world I thought that it must be for the purposes of that world that we had met. I never doubted that our meeting was for his good and mine. I had not been looking for a lover—indeed my life at that time was calm and industrious enough—nor indeed was Gavin ever to be my lover. What was between us was something else altogether, though I loved him as much as, being what I am, I am able to use so great a word. The experience had rather, as it seemed, to do with poetry than with any personal fulfilment.

A few days after that first meeting we met at lunch, with Tambi and possibly other people present. I happened to raise my eyes and saw that Gavin was looking at me. The eyes which had formerly seemed closed were now open; and he held mine in a long look, as if testing me; and I saw who he was. In this century it must seem strange to speak of the mystery of the eyes, from which, in former times, it was said that the soul looks out. Dante speaks of beholding, in the eyes of Beatrice, the reflection of the mystery of the two natures of the Divine Humanity; and is not this still the mystery to be read in human eyes? The living light of the eyes is that of the soul's country, not the body's. I tend to avoid looking into people's eyes, or allowing them to look into mine; for those who look into my eyes, so I feel, can see me; and I seldom wish to be seen; but by Gavin I wished to be seen and known.

He told me, early in our acquaintance, that he could not love me with erotic desire, and why; yet in the very telling it seemed to me there was love. He was, he explained to me, homosexual. This did not seem to me to matter, for I understood that I was nevertheless necessary to him; 'Every man needs a woman in his life,' he said; and I thought I was that woman for him. And I, having found the one being in the world who seemed to be of my own lonely species thought that at last all sorrow was over, that I had come at last to that for which I had been born. I too was unmarriage-

17

able, though for different reasons, as I had learned to my cost. The poet in me could never marry. Now it seemed that miracle—the operation of some order other than that of this world—had brought together two people who, neither fitting the conventional, or indeed the natural pattern, were perfectly and providentially fitted to one another.

Both pride and the fear of being hurt once more would have made it impossible for me to seek acquaintance with any man; or indeed with anyone at all—I never, in friendship, made the first advance. But it was he who sought me out, he who seemed to need me; for at that time I was strong, he weak; I was happy, he wretched; my life had at last achieved some sort of stability, his was in ruins. Gavin had come to London with the idea of making a career for himself as a painter of portraits after losing all his patrimony on his shark-fishing venture on the Isle of Soay, the little low isle that lies to the south of Skye under the Cuillin. At the same time he had suffered a personal unhappiness. Soon he had told me all the story. My defences were disarmed: I thought I could help him. (And that thought was not all generosity; there was in it both pride and timidity).

Had Gavin wished to be my lover I would have been happy; but what drew me to him was nothing bodily, but rather the radiance his presence had for me always. He was for me what Gay Taylor used to call 'the man of light'; seeing him, as I did, with the eyes of my spirit rather than with my bodily eyes. He seemed, besides, a part of myself, as if the 'one consciousness' lived us both. If I were to describe him, as I can describe friends less near, it would not be from that place from which I knew him. I could, of course, do so; but that would be his outward personality. An Indian friend once pointed out to me that in the *Ramayana*, Sita, questioned about her husband, was silent; from which the querent deduced their relationship: he was too near to be described. And for some such reason, even though I could describe Gavin, I may not do so without violation of some sacred reticence.

18

All seemed a miracle, unsought, undeserved, and I vowed deeply to the world that had drawn aside the veil to keep faith with what I had seen and known. Seeing his need, I who had at that time strength and no sorrow offered myself to that world, to take upon myself Gavin's suffering as the price of his release from it. I was sincere, though I had no idea of the burden I then took voluntarily upon myself; but had I done so it would have made no difference, for I knew the task for mine. It is, besides, easy to make light of pain we have not yet felt.

After my return from Northumberland and my epiphany of the Tree I felt that I must above all write poems. For a long time I had written none; but I believed that the 'other' mind, in unveiling a portion of its mystery, had summoned me to my task. Other and better poets than I—Coleridge in *Kubla Khan*, Keats in the *Hyperion* fragments—tell of the awakening of imaginative recollection, the true poetic initiation, which is the soul's remembering not of its mortal but of its immortal history; not of individual knowledge but of the one consciousness, the Platonic anamnesis. Plunged, therefore, into those living currents and eddies, I thought that I too had been made an initiate, then, of the immortal world of the imagination, once and for ever; I thought those doors would stand ever open for me to come and go at will. I thought that I would live for ever under the branches of that Tree. Such insights that unite, in Yeats' words, 'for certain moments the sleeping and the waking mind' are not attained, but given; it was for me to receive. I thought, then, that I had reached at last the threshold, that here my task began.

As soon as my children had gone back to school, I went to Helen Sutherland to write the poems I now felt I must write—the first, as I believed and hoped, of many more to come from that inexhaustible source.

It was in the same white room at Cockley Moor, looking over to High Street, with one small field of Martindale visible among the folds of the fells; the room where I have written so many poems, the room where I wrote the poems I called *Northumbrian Sequence*, that I returned to write, when all was over, this record. I looked back, now, over all that was still to come, over seven years and more, 'beginning, middle and end,' those three phases of all completed events. It was another Greek who said 'beginnings are better than endings', but that again is only as it appears to us: to the divine agents who know the end before the beginning, who create beginnings for the sake of ends unguessed, it may be otherwise.

I had at this time known Gavin only for two, or at most three, weeks. I had not told him of the Tree, still less of the poems I intended to write; I did not myself know what form they would take. We had indeed spoken of our childhood, his and mine, those worlds so strangely interwoven; of how my mother, in the Kielder kirk, had sat behind his mother, admiring her coils of shining hair; and of the uncle who had died so young, in whose room the birds flew free; and of many things we both had seen and known, though not together. He had restored to me that which in revisiting Bavington I had looked for but not found; and I had perhaps done the like for him, reminding him of a time before his own entangled troubles. While I was in Cumberland, writing my poems, he was visiting friends in the country elsewhere; and he too wrote a poem. We met, after our return to London, and I showed him my *Northumbrian Sequence*; and he then said, 'everyone will think I copied my poem from yours', and showed me what he had written. Neither in metre nor in language did his poem resemble mine, but every image, and the sequence of the images, was the same as in the fifth poem in my own sequence; for he too had described the Tree, as I had also seen it.

Had we evoked, each in the other, the archetype of Eden because the bond between us was the world of childhood? Yet how explain the identity of the images, even when these departed from tradition? How explain why each had chosen a rowan-tree drawing its waters from a dark river, and

20

bearing fruit which was eaten by a bird, whose song then rose from the tree as its highest transformation? Neither Gavin's tree nor mine grew in a walled garden, and in neither was there a serpent, nor any other emblem of evil. The only difference was that in his tree there was no sleeper at the foot, and his bird was not a blackbird but an ousel. As a naturalist he had thought of a bird he knew to haunt the rowan; while my blackbird was perhaps literary, being Merlin; for the vision seemed above all to concern poetry, the oracular bird-voice.

Were the two poems the result of telepathy—'only' telepathy? That would be mysterious enough; but I do not believe this to be so. That place we saw was not of my making, nor of his, as dreams are of our weaving, but one of the archetypal objects of visionary knowledge. How else explain the unvarying character of the elements of that vision, which many have seen, described and painted, differing in this aspect or in that, but in essence always the same? The vision was, besides, so seemingly impersonal, without any bearing on our own concerns, its elements not stitched together, as in ordinary dreams, from daily odds and ends. I thought we had been greatly blessed in meeting on that holy ground, by the Tree of Life.

That either of us should break faith with the mystery which we had shared seemed to me inconceivable; I imagined that we should remain, to the end of our lives, as we were then; and perhaps we should have done so. But one part of the Eden myth I forgot to apply either to Gavin or to myself—the Fall; so inconceivable did it seem that any who had seen the eternal beauty could betray it.

I made a vow that this time I would do nothing wrong, nothing not in obedience to the senders of that vision. I wanted only to give, to pour out upon Gavin the help and consolation for which he at that time turned to me. He once said to me, in those days, 'It is as if a goddess had turned her head and looked at me'; but if there was in my sense of a boundless power of inspiration at that time an element of spiritual

21

pride I was not aware of it, for all seemed to be given from that other kingdom. If I felt in myself goddess-strength, I knew myself to be only instrumental. At that time indeed I seemed to possess a magical power to help Gavin. It was my custom to write small prayers upon slips of paper and place these behind the ear of an Indo-Chinese Buddha; and so many strange and beautiful small miracles seemed at that time to happen that I came to imagine, as I think he did also, that I had a magical power to help him. I seemed to be living rather in that world than in this; and perhaps for a while I really had found unawares some magical secret. Yet in retrospect I see that my belief that I was the giver was all illusion: it was I who through Gavin received riches untold.

As for the painting, that was soon abandoned; I told Gavin that he wrote better than he painted. He talked of Soay and the romance of his disastrous shark-fishery venture, and I said he should write the story. This he did, reading me each section as it was written. He would telephone me at any hour of the day and I would obediently and gladly go, listen, praise, criticize. I was still, for him, sufficiently Tambi's 'great poet' for my encouragement to seem worth having. When as a writer he rose to fame I still saw him as that younger brother, for whose success I was glad; but I always knew myself to be stronger than he, and possessed of greater knowledge and power. I knew, therefore, that the responsibility of our relationship lay principally, if not altogether, with me.

Such was my sense of kinship with him that I sometimes half imagined that we had been in some former life brother and sister, or in some other such close bond of kinship; I never imagined us as having been lovers, much less as married. He told me that in my pride especially I did remind him of his own family. Gavin, at all events, understood that it was pride that had kept me from coming to terms with the world; that it was more fitting to pride to wear shabby clothes and to wonder often enough how the milkman was to be paid than to sell that pride for money to the British

22

Council (for which I had worked for a time) or the like. To Gavin I did not need to explain such things, which for him were self-evident; for he saw, in that respect, who I was. Being himself an aristocrat what others have called my 'arrogance' did not irk him; he felt no reproach in the pride of others.

It is well to know the meaning of the mystic hours; well indeed; but how are mortals to know the meaning of immortal life? When we are awakened to those unguessed depths in ourselves where, it is said, unfallen man in Eden walked in the divine presence, we are in a world of purposes other than our own; other, at all events, than those of our once-born selves. Supposing it were to be said that so to meet by the Tree of Life is to fall in love, what is love, into which we fall—or rise? Some say that love is always a disguised self-interest; others, that 'God is love'; I do not know which mine was. It was, in either case, the heart of life. What has such love to do with the crude animal instinct by which the species is continued? The soul has other ends, another nature. As an animal, indeed, man is most detestable; yet the real object of Freudianism, behaviourism and the like, is a regression to the animal from which mankind has from the beginning of our humanity struggled to rise. Yet is it not our 'nature' to attempt the supernatural? Whether the *Divina Commedia* be an insight into reality, or a creation of it, such are the realities which belong to man, as man. Alexander the Great who was Aristotle's pupil is said to have said that man was never less human than in the act of sex; and the young world-conqueror returned from India bringing with him a new *guru*, a Brahman forest-dweller, who remained with him until his death; the Rishi is always the last teacher. The human animal may afterwards choose Plato and Plotinus for friend; but the direction of our growth is irreversible; for those who have glimpsed another order, there is scarcely even a question of 're-nouncing' carnality: we are drawn by our strongest love, to the most desirable. I, who in my youth was caught up in

23

erotic passion and would have sacrificed all else to it, now thought carnal desire a small thing to forgo for the sake of a deeper love. It seemed to me that to have stood with another soul before that Tree must constitute a sacred bond. Marriage, lacking that dimension, had not seemed to me a binding relationship; but this, rooted in paradisal ground, seemed to me eternally binding; and yet not so much to one another as each of us to that mystery on whose surface individual lives form and vanish. There are those who have travelled farther than I to whom it will be clear that what I took for the end was only the beginning of the journey the soul must take; but I tremble still at the austerities of those for whom all personal ties are renounced; as some (being still as I was in the years of sexual passion) may tremble at the thought of the renunciation of the mere flesh. But I can tell only my own story. By some happy chance we had eluded ourselves, and we were there.

The country through the looking-glass is entered, as everybody knows, by walking the other way. But to walk the other way is less easy than it sounds, for who has ever not desired to taste the heavenly fruit with earthly lips? Long ago at Bavington I remember having read, Heaven knows where, a story that must have been written by some theosophist. It told of two people, a man and a woman, who met in dreams. Each set out over the world to find the other and at last they met, married—and lost the vision. Sorrowing they went in search of an Indian sage who said to them, 'You were given the seed of the greatest of all trees, but you exchanged it for earthly happiness: you have not been wise.' When I was a child (a colour print of Rossetti's painting of Dante and Beatrice hung in the drawing-room) I used to think 'poor Dante, how sad it was that he could never marry Beatrice whom he loved,' not understanding that he was permitted to meet her in the only country where such lovers can meet. For the life of the soul, its native country is, as Boehme says, 'in another principle'; and to enter that principle, and still more to remain in it, is always hard. So

24

it was, fallen creatures as we were, that 'we had the experience but missed the meaning'.

For I forgot that it is only as poet that the poet can enter Eden, forgot that the once-born betrays the twice-born, that the mortal self must weep outside the locked gates with the rest of fallen humanity. Coleridge must live on with his sick body and broken heart; Keats, to whom Moneta brought the lyre of Apollo, must die, pining for Fanny Brawne. In Plato's Garden of the Muses, the poets, 'winged, light and volatile' draw honey and milk from divine fountains 'which they cannot do when in their sober minds'. Blake wrote that 'If the Spectator could enter into these Images in his Imagination, approaching them on the Fiery Chariot of his Contemplative Thought . . . or could make a Friend and Companion of one of these Images of wonder, which always intreats him to leave mortal things (as he must know), then he would arise from his Grave, then would he meet the Lord in the Air, and then he would be happy.' Blake's 'as he must know' is not unjustified, since such insights bring their own knowledge with them, tell of their own nature; yet he too knew that 'while we are in the world of mortality, we must suffer'. We are not in Paradise because we have seen one 'image of wonder'. And yet, merely to know that world exists is a happiness so great that the mere knowledge outweighs any possible suffering: and, as another said, 'Life is suffering'.

The once-born have sufferings of their own, because of the inevitable distance between any wish and its fulfilment; yet wish and fulfilment exist within realizable terms: as, when we are hungry, a meal is a possibility, even to the starving. If we starve it is not because this world offers no possible satisfaction for our hunger; and the right conduct of the world of the once-born (the political virtues) consists, precisely, of making bread available to the hungry, shelter to the houseless. But the bread and the wine that feed the body, in whatever abundance we may possess them, cannot satisfy the soul; though positivists believe that this

is so. Once I said something of the kind to George Orwell—
that those who have riches of the mind have less need than
others of material wealth; to which he replied that the
converse is also true: a witty retort, and for politicians
shrewd wisdom, but still untrue in the last resort, as even
politicians must discover. For those who have once seen the
world beyond, or within, the world (which is, for humanity,
that place or state towards which we are impelled to travel,
with an urgency no less than that which, according to the
Darwinian mythology, drove amphibians from water to
land) there are awakened desires which this world cannot
fulfil. Therefore, some starve in the midst of plenty, and
some enjoy plenty in the midst of poverty.

Yet suffering was never farther from my thoughts. I wrote
many poems and thought to write many more; for I seemed
then to stand upon some marvellous threshold. Sorrow
seemed something for every past; for who, having once
glimpsed the beauty of the world behind the world could
ever lose the joy of that knowledge; as such, and irrespective
of what might happen to one's self.

Gay Taylor compared Gavin's horoscope with mine and
was less confident; certainly there was a bond, but it might
prove rather of sorrow than of joy; for the sun of my natal
map was in the same degree as Gavin's Saturn; and though
I might pour solar beams into his shadow, his shadow ob-
scured my sun. But I did not care, so long as I was to be light
to his darkness. I felt then that I had riches inexhaustible to
bestow and strength to carry that shadowy burden. As for
the possible effects of dark Pluto who, in my natal map, is in
conjunction with my sun, little was known, Gay said, about
Pluto: she could not tell. I would not have believed that the
lonely wanderer in outer darkness could encompass the
loss of Paradise both to Gavin and to myself. I had not read
the myths attentively enough, or, like Plato's souls when
they chose 'patterns of lives', looked into the fate I chose
with the caution of Odysseus; but it is too late when fate is
already chosen; and that, Plato says, is before we are born.

Meanwhile it seemed that my meeting with Gavin had healed every old wound and made of my fragmented life a whole. My long flight had brought me back at last to all I had ever loved, to the roots from which I had been torn away. The reality of my life, first and last, was my ancestral inheritance: seemingly meagre, it proved now to be richer than I had known. End had met beginning, yet the full circle of return raised past and present onto another plane. For now I had been given back, as an evolved person, what I had as a child lived in country simplicity. Now even the long wanderings seemed to have been not without purpose; the country child, the student of biology, the poet, all in my life that had belonged to what in truth I am, had been restored like a lost kingdom.

Not only the fields of childhood did we seem to share; Gavin was a naturalist, and had taken a way I had once dreamed of following. For him, as for me, such knowledge of nature was less a branch of learning than an experience of imagination. Certain saints have been able to speak to the creatures in their own language, communicating with the one life which is in them as it is in us; St. Francis' birds, or St. Cuthbert's seals. This secret knowledge of nature was Gavin's gift, as poetry was mine; his grey-lag geese, his springer spaniel, Johnnie. As my poetry stemmed from a vision of nature, so was his participation in nature a kind of poetry. He, too, had been brought up on the English poets, and most of Palgrave's *Golden Treasury* he seemed to know by heart.

Martindale too seemed given back; for that also had belonged to the country of imagination which we shared; the same wilderness, the same birds and flowers and brown water flowing over stones under alder and birch, speaking everywhere and always the same language. I was glad, now, that Alastair had never entered that valley, for now that virgin country too I brought to Gavin, bestowing on him all the lands of my imagination. It had been the ancestral voices, then, whose clamour had so summoned me, reminded me, filled me with such overwhelming longing for my own place; but if Alastair* was moulded of ancestral clay, Gavin was the spirit of my lost inheritance.

I now understood that there is a fidelity far different from any kind imposed from without, even by the strongest act of resolution. In love it is as if the timeless soul knows all its past and future and what it is. In the light of that knowledge we do not need to promise lifelong fidelity, for it is given; we are ourselves the given, not the givers. Because the experience of the Tree, of the shared vision of paradise, had seemed mutual, I thought that Gavin, as well as I, was thus committed. Had Gavin wished to be my lover, I would not have refused; I would not have refused him anything love could ask or give. But since this was not asked I was even glad to make to love the sacrifice of sexual desire; only to love, indeed, can such a sacrifice have any meaning; and this too seemed fitting, and to belong to my fate, as a poet. I was glad, even, to be free of physical involvement, to be among those lovers *che sono gentili, e non sono pure femmine.*

But to every love there are limits; yet since the limit set to mine seemed in no way to conflict with what Gavin asked of me, or with those areas of our lives which we had in common, he never, I think, discerned that limit in me: I would not have married Gavin; for this would have compromised the daimon. I would not, in any case, now, have married anyone; and I thought myself greatly blessed in having been sent, as it seemed by that divine providence that cares for the needs of all, a relationship which was of the only kind of which I was capable. Gavin, too, I believed, had been no less fortunate in finding a woman who, in loving him, was willing to forgo sexual love. Therefore our relationship seemed to me honourable according to the values both of this world and the other. But if I knew what my reservation was, I held it not as a criticism of Gavin but as one more reason for gratitude to the 'one consciousness' who had sent to two unusual people what was exactly

* See *The Land Unknown*

28

according to the need and capacity of each. We had each, besides, our pride of caste: he as an aristocrat, I as a poet; and this, far from impairing our harmony, was an element in it.

For such love there is, besides, none of those pains of separation from which the body suffers; for wherever Gavin might be, or I might be, we were (as it seemed) present to one another. (It is strange that of this aspect of love so little has been written; *Voss*, by Patrick White, is the only novel known to me which makes a love of this kind central.) I had ceased to be alone; for absence was no interruption of the sense of continuous relationship; his thoughts turned towards me as mine to him; we were at all times attuned; or so I thought; for what ground for jealousy could there be in a relationship grounded in reality itself? To be unfaithful in that world is to be unfaithful to that world; and therefore to what we in our essence are.

I was no more blind to Gavin's faults than I was impressed by his skills and talents. Gavin, touchingly humble, perhaps did not understand this. I remember his saying, on one occasion, that he would lose his good looks with age; and on another seeming to think that I valued him for his talents. Heaven knows, on a simple level of companionship to be with him was always a delight. However I might harbour some mistrust or resentment when Gavin was not there, all melted in the joy of being in his company. He was, above all, the best person in the world to laugh with at the happy comedy of life, as two people can who share the little daily things of which relationships are made. How different it had been with Alastair, whom I only imagined I loved when he was *not* there. But no mortal best or worst can be commensurable with what love sees; at best the outer personality can be irradiated by, at worst cut off from, the essence which, in its very nature, we love. The former can cause happiness, the latter pain, or, at worst, grief to the lover; but it cannot in any way disillusion a love that is not in its nature an illusion, but a truer insight. To call love

29

blind is to reverse the truth: which is that only love has insight into another person's essential being. Love is in any case no less a task than a privilege; the task is implicit in the love. It is no one's duty *to* love for no one can at will evoke that mystery; but love is its own duty.

Above all, through Gavin, I could at last make peace with my parents. The long flight from them, the struggle to escape, the sense of being continually dragged back and down into Ilford, had never ceased; there had been times of respite, but always it was there, every new wound reopening the old. In order to survive I had hardened my heart against them. My father I had fought on equal terms, indeed, mind with mind. My mother's weapons had been those of love; her tears had pursued me, the devouring longing she had for me to love her, to be her daughter, to take her into my life. I had fought her off with weapons more deadly than those I had used against my father, hating and fearing her terrible suffering sorrowful unsatisfied love. To have my parents in my life was, defenceless as I had been, more than I could have carried and survived. My father's moral disapproval, however justified, had at all times been at cross-purposes with the deepest springs of my own life; and I could never have satisfied my mother's hunger for all she had been denied—she would have dragged me under with her, like a drowning swimmer. Or so I thought; all who are unhappy must in some measure shrink from their parents' intrusion into the regions of sorrow; and I had never forgiven mine for (as it had seemed to me for so long that the thought had become habitual and all but unalterable), laying a ban on my womanhood, forbidding me to love. Of a Platonic love, my father could not disapprove; and now, my heart being healed, I could forgive them; and also I felt that at last I had gained the victory on behalf of the caged winged spirit which had inhabited my mother and me. The roots of my love for Gavin seemed to go back beyond myself, as if I were enacting a fate laid upon me by my mother, and perhaps by even earlier ancestors, from time immemorial. I understood my mother, now; understood that it was she who had made me a poet, that I was the custodian of all her unenacted possibilities. I understood that her tears and grief from which I had shrunk from my earliest childhood were the measure of those unrealized energies of love and of imagination. I knew that in loving Gavin I loved as she would have wished; even as she might herself once have woven round one or another of those young golden lords whom she had seen so near at hand but yet as far above her as if they had belonged to the race of the gods, her dreams. Even if she had had no such dream, yet it is true that the cement of the feudal world was the people's being as it were in love with the bright illustrious ones whose physical beauty and whose deeds were adorned with poetry. I could see my mother, again, as in her radical nature she was; a hawk with wild bird's eyes, and a wild bird's clipped wings. Gavin himself saw in my mother what I saw; saw the hawk-soul; for he too was one of that winged race. He brought to tea his own mother of the shining coils, and the two old ladies compared memories.

As to all my life between, it fell away from me as if it had never been, or had been a long dream from which I had now awakened. I felt myself absolved of my life, and perhaps was so. I had indeed through weakness or through blind flight injured both myself and others, involved my external life in many falsities; but I had kept faith with some central truth. For that priceless thing I had torn down my life again and again and been like a sword to all who had come near me. I felt myself absolved because how could a vision of the eternal beauty be given, if not by that world itself? Such things cannot be stolen. The only truth of my life had been the truth of my poetry to the living imagination; and Gavin as it seemed, had come to me as by a miraculous act of the daimons themselves, unsought, not even wished for. How natural, how inevitable does supreme happiness seem, how utterly do we forget all else as if it had never been; whereas sorrow, however long it may continue and with whatever

31

fortitude it may be borne (and I have never lacked fortitude) seems always alien. Never this, the soul cries, not for this was I born. But every joy seems a homecoming, a return to what forever is.

I knew, of course, that Gavin was less committed than I to the inner ground of imagination. We all, insofar as we live in both worlds, are at times more aware of the one or the other, so that the one or the other seems for the time more real. Gavin, I realized, was often intent upon the ends of this world, and was at such times even prepared to use the riches of the other world as a means to trivial ends; a reversal of the due order of values. He had found some-where a book, made by some Victorian botanist, of red and green seaweeds, beautifully pressed and mounted; each species—some of them rare—identified in a fine old learned script; such a book as I as a botanist would once have wished to make; it had about it the quality which for me belonged to the manuscript books in which my poems are written. It was a book of great imaginative quality, the lovely delicate algae patterns themselves as eloquent as poems. Yet when his first book was about to appear, Gavin ripped the sea-weeds from their pages to make a window-display in a book-shop. I felt as if I had myself been ripped and torn, as if I were those fine learned beautiful pages sacrificed to a hand-to-mouth end, in ignorance. Clearly enough the daimon warned me that I too might be made the means to some trivial end; warned me that the sin, in that case, would be mine no less than his for allowing this to happen; more, indeed, since I had the knowledge he lacked. Yet I believed that because our bond was in the ground of Paradise that never, never could Gavin behave so to me. I believed also that because the world we had seen is more real than this world of shadows, that it must also prevail.

(Now, in 1976, I am revising this record, written fifteen years ago; more than twenty years after the story I am tell-ing. And I can now see many things differently. Love—love, yes, I 'loved' Gavin with my whole soul, but what of that

32

soul? For I recall—why did I not record this when in so white-hot a passion of grief I wrote my story—that Gavin too was warned. He was sitting with me in my room at 9 Paultons Square, that pleasant room with books and a fire in the hearth and a pear-tree outside the window, inherited from Cooie Lane—and there must have been some jar between us; for I remember that over Gavin's face came a look of dismay and he said, 'A *spider*, Kathleen!'—a great spider had crawled out from under my chair. A spider, the female devourer.)

*

As the one consciousness brings about the meeting of persons, so it changes the landscape of our lives in correspondence with interior states; and it was to Gavin that I owed my last return to the earthly paradise.

Gavin, from the wreck of his fortunes, had kept one thing: a small, shepherd's house, on a friend's estate on a wild coast of the Western Highlands; and beyond the house, a group of little islets on the largest of which was a lighthouse.

> . . . an island salt and bare,
> The haunt of orcs and seales and sea-mew's clang.

Into such an isle, so Milton tells, the mount of Paradise was changed when the man and the woman were driven away. Doubtless to Milton, whose own paradise was that Italy he had visited as a young man, such isles must have seemed, as Thule to the Romans, the fittest symbol of uttermost exile. But he wrote more truly than he knew; for the orcs and seals and sea-mews on those salt bare isles live on in the inviolate places. The fine intangible essence of that lost country is in the very air, more sweetly fragrant with the scent of sea-weed, bog myrtle and birch leaves than Milton's

> Groves whose rich trees wept odorous gums and balm.

It is even said by those who live in the Western Isles—and this Milton can scarcely have known—that the Gaelic speech was the language of Eden. Nor could he have known

33

how thin the veil which there divides the visible from the radiant 'other' land whose image is mirrored on those silver seas. The very light is like a quality of the imagination—the same imagination that sings in those ancient pentatonic and hexatonic melodies that seem the pure utterance of the one mind which casts the light on the sea and raises the hills like visions.

Here was the country 'over the border', the boundless country of mountain and sea and isles of which Northumberland and the distant Cheviots had been only a foreshadowing, a dignity of nature as vast as pride, with yet such tenderness of sheltered glen, of birch and mossy stone, and everywhere the freedom of waters flowing, the freedom of the lives of the wild birds and wild creatures in their sanctuaries. My mother's country, though she had never herself known it.

Is there a spiritual geography, are there certain places upon the earth which are more, or less, attuned to certain modes of consciousness? And if so, do such qualities belong to the earth itself, to certain qualities of light, or sound, or scent, or rock formation? Is there a natural magic, and elemental spirits who inhabit certain places, or kinds of place? Or do people of a certain cast of mind impart to the land their own qualities? It seems not to be true, as Wordsworth sometimes seems to imply, that 'nature' can impart a culture; and the people of Cumberland and Northumberland (whatever they were in the Border Ballad days) are prosaic enough. Hardy's people had a sense of history, yet only Hardy has made poetry of their lives. But in the Highlands I found people who possessed a culture; a culture not only deeper than that of the Northumbrians of my childhood, but also than positivist Cambridge. Oral tradition still transmitted, not merely the history of the race and its memories, but certain ancient attitudes and values lost to the technological present. I was already at this time, though still blindly, seeking for the lost thread of another tradition altogether than the materialist civilization dominant in

34

England; dominant no less in poetry and the arts (as I had discovered to my cost in Cambridge) than in science and technology. My friend Herbert Read continued to believe that its arts can save that civilization; but I had come to see in its arts only another symptom of the spiritual disease of which it is dying.

It was in the June following my meeting with Gavin that Winifred Nicholson and I went for the first time to Eigg; she to paint, I to write. 'You can see the flash of my lighthouse from the *sgurr*,' Gavin had said; and for me, Eigg was above all an isle from which I could see the flash of his light. But that is the character of the Isles where summit and skerry are seamarks known to every boatman and shepherd, and the unchanging scene into which life is woven through the generations, from isle to isle, and so is likely to be so long as the mountains of Rhum and Canna's Compass Hill stand against the winds and the seas. Indeed are not all Scots bound into nationhood by a landscape of isles and mountains known to all? And were we not all once so bound to the earth itself, for countless generations before we were driven into the exile of the modern urban scene, ever-shifting and impermanent, where all sense of continuity of the generations is lost? 'I don't know how humanity stands it,' as Ezra Pound said.

On midsummer eve, I remember, we climbed the hill for the first time to the point where the road looks down to Cleadale, the crofters' village facing to the west. The long evening light was magical; Winifred painted a picture of Rhum, which I was not able to see until the paint had dried and the multitudes of adhering midges could be brushed off. From below we heard two girls singing as they gathered up their washing from the machair. Those lovely voices heard in the absence of all mechanical noise, where only the cries of sheep and birds and the sound of the sea accompanied their singing is something not to be heard any more; for the televison sets have reached the outermost isles, and the sounds there now are what they are elsewhere. I did not

35

know then that I was hearing for almost the last time something so simple and so familiar to mankind from the beginning. But it was not so much the past that we seemed there to enter, but the permanent, the enduring norm, the familiar.

We had taken rooms in the somewhat bleak manse; but we were lent an empty house at Kildonan, site of an early monastic settlement. Each day, Winifred painted in one room, while I wrote in the other. Happy, productive days. But whereas for Winifred, whose roots are so deep in the past of Cumberland, it was an adventure into a beautiful strange land, for me it was like a recovery of a lost identity, a re-grafting to an old root, though already long severed when I was born. For our tea we boiled water drawn from the near-by spring on just such a kitchen range as I had known at Bavington. Of course I was not really returning home; it was only as if; yet Gavin's lighthouse flashing its message made it seem so.

On Eigg that summer, and later on the mainland and on other Isles, I came to know people whose simplicity of life was permeated with an essential quality of which poetry is the natural speech; Homer might have sung in those kitchens by turf fires, with shepherds' dogs under the table and the wooden chairs drawn back round the walls. On Eigg there was a bard—Hugh MacKinnon—who composed his verses stretched at length on the kitchen bench, a cap over his eyes; a tradition handed down from the Bardic schools where the *fili* composed their verses lying on their beds and in darkness. In such company I found myself not, as in England, too much a poet, but not poet enough, for I could neither sing nor recite, as all did here, their learning all stored in their memory. I had been away too long by several generations, although indeed in my grandmother's kitchen people had sung—all my mother's sisters had sweet voices and memories stored with the songs of the Lowlands. In the house of Hugh MacKinnon I heard stories of things done and suffered by men and women whose houses now

36

were just green mounds. For the bard is the guardian of memories, and the maker of stories that still brought grief and joy and laughter to the descendants of those vanished ancestors. There were stories, too, that included the inner, the supernatural event; I first met the 'Celtic twilight' not through books but at the source itself; a privilege the more treasured as it was unsought.

If I had not my own story to tell—sadly modern, an outsider's story—I could retell, though with less artistry than he, many of Hugh MacKinnon's stories of people and events of that borderland between memory and history that the imagination of Highland people still inhabits; the borderland, also, between inner and outer worlds. But the telling of such stories is not my purpose, except insofar as they contribute, in some degree, to the picture I have been trying to compose of what a life is, and what a world. I will tell only one, for the story moved me deeply at the time, and seemed to belong, at the time and still more later, to the mystery into which I had entered, to find myself in the deep waters where thoughts are realities.

The story was a recent one, as most stories of the supernatural are; there is no need to go back into the past to find such things, which are common, if not everyday occurrences in the Celtic Twilight. Some cattle-men had been sitting in a bar in Oban, and up to one of the men—who belonged to a certain sept, I think of the Macdonalds— came a grey bitch and stood at his knee. Several men saw the dog; and the man to whom it had come said, 'That is a sign of my death.' He showed no sign of illness at the time, but within a week he was dead. The young priest (now well known and respected from Fort William to Barra and Eriskay) who administered the last rites bore witness to the truth of the story. For it was well known that the grey bitch appears before the death of members of that sept, sometimes to the person about to die, sometimes to a relation. I was told that another man had seen the dog on his doorstep when a brother had died, without his knowledge, in another

37

country; as others will see a white bird, or the death-coach. Thought-forms no doubt; but what is a thought-form?

The story the bard of the Isle of Eigg told of the origin of the grey dog may be a later rationalization of some more ancient belief. It tells of a young Macdonald who went away, like so many impoverished lairds of the seventeenth and eighteenth centuries, to fight as a mercenary in the army of (probably) Gustavus Adolphus. The young man had a grey bitch to whom he was deeply attached; and after his departure the dog grieved and at last left the house altogether. (Here I will add that I have often noticed that dogs, in Highland conversation are treated as persons, their deeds and characters discussed as on a par with human beings; cats are not 'people' in this sense.) After some years the master returned, and asked for his dog. He was told that she was living on a certain islet on the loch, and went to seek her. But the grey bitch had raised, on the island, a brood of puppies. When he came there it so happened that the bitch was (according to Hugh Mackinnon's phrase echoing back to a world that vanished many centuries ago), 'on the hunting-hill'; and the young dogs, being wild, set upon the young man and tore him to pieces. When the bitch came back and found her master dead, 'her heart was broken'; (the phrase as the story was told seemed neither sentimental nor figurative; it is felt to be no less appropriate to dog or hind than to humanity) and she disappeared never to return to any human dwelling. It is she who appears when a man in that sept is to die.

Another frontier that melts away in that Twilight is the barrier between man and animal; mankind and nature altogether. The natural world is presumed to be possessed of life and consciousness similar to our own; never questioned by that part of mankind living close to the natural world, where it has not been forgotten that we are ourselves but a part of that nature. I had come at last to a country where the world is experienced continuously as if informed with life and meaning. All those works of Vedanta and

38

Cabbala and the Neoplatonists that I had been studying in the British Museum saw the nature of things in terms consistent with the experience of these survivors of the archaic Celtic world. Those few who, like myself at odds with current ideologies, have worked our way through Berkeley and Plotinus, Boehme and the alchemists and all the learned books, reach a knowledge which, even so, does not readily transform itself into an experience, informing the whole of life, and embodying itself, as here, in the symbolic images of an unwritten poetry.

For so these stories were to me. But what was I but a stranger and an alien, one of those whose very presence destroys that rare medium in which the thought-forms of a tribe or race form and dissolve? It was Gavin, not I, who belonged to that legendary land.

It was in the early spring of the following year that Gavin first lent me his house. Again, Winifred was my companion. I still have one of the paintings she made there, that I can still enter, sometimes, as if it were the place itself. I first saw that house in the early evening, the sun pouring gold across the sea from beyond Skye into the bay; and the rowan-tree before the house (for there was a rowan) just opening the white of the young leaves that enclose the blossom. Often I have seen the little ferny hill beyond in that peculiar light within the circle of the rainbow which seems to transform earthly green into its unearthly archetype, such beauty does it shed. Primroses grew on that brae, and later in the year heather and thyme and golden asphodel among the bog-myrtle and the gold tormentil. But it is not vegetation that makes Eden, nor the fall of water flowing, nor rowan- nor apple-tree in bloom; it is the power of entering that invisible closed gate which is everywhere and nowhere. I have known the natural world closed, and I have known it open; and perhaps no dust is too mean to shine with that unfallen radiance. Yet I have walked in flowery Italy, in Greece, in the virgin woods of America, and no-where found that gate.

Many times thereafter I was to live in that house; alone, after that first visit with Winifred. Never was I there with Gavin; yet, living in his house, seeing his sky over me, the spaces of his sea, those near hills and far mountains which were the regions of his imagination; his green linnet in the alder by the burn, his sanderling and plover running on the shore, his tern wheeling over their nests on the furthest rocky islet, his eider floating on the waves, I lived like Psyche in the house of love, alone yet not alone. In the pool of his waterfall I bathed, on his beaches I gathered shells and stones written with the strange language of the sea.

He lent his house, in those years, to none but me; and, as I thought, as if in his absence he wished me to experience his world for him. I saw for him, touched and smelled and heard all as for him, as if every wheeling bird, every radiance of sun or moon on water, every sound of wind or sea or waterfall I was hearing and seeing and touching and knowing for him; or for both of us, perhaps; for the 'one consciousness'. I forgot that his house was not mine, for I was there as it were as an extension of himself, to love all he loved because it was his; was, indeed, himself, a region of his consciousness. I felt it to be my task to enrich and transmute for him his world into poetry.

Near the house, in what had once been a garden (though so long overgrown with fine turf that only the cross made by the intersecting paths could now be seen) there grew the rowan-tree; and I can remember days when I have sat under the blue windy sky, leaning against the silver trunk, looking up into the boundless blue and thinking, what miracle, what unimaginable blessedness to be here and now at the place on earth I most desire to be; by Gavin's rowan.

One midsummer's eve, in the long gloaming, Mary, the wife of the lighthouse-keeper who lived in a cottage on the hill close above the islets, walked with me up the burn, with the setting sun shedding its gold among the birch-leaves as we climbed. By the high waterfall where the burn drops from the treeless level down among the birches that

40

fringe its lower pools and falls, we came suddenly upon a place where not one, nor a few, but many hundreds of globe-flowers were blooming. Each green-gold flower seemed to hold in its sphere of petals the light of that mid-summer evening. Yet had we not been there together, Mary and I, and both seen those golden flowers, I might not have believed after that they had ever been there; for the next year there were none; not even one; nor have been ever again.

And one day I went to gather rowan-berries, and leaned from a little rocky crag, my head among the branches and leaves; and I saw a blackbird there. It did not move, but remained quiet as if unafraid in its own place; and as at Martindale I had experienced the life of the hyacinth, so—almost—my consciousness seemed one with the bird-thought, the pattern of leaves, the sense of sanctuary where the bird's invisible comings and goings were woven into the tree like a living texture I could sense as some subtle field of vital force; the sense of the bird-soul in the tree, intimate and inviolate sanctuary of the *spiritus mundi*.

I do not know whether such happiness as I then knew is the rarest or the commonest of earthly things; broadcast as the light, as flowers, as leaves, as common as heather, asphodel, bog-cotton and brown butterflies on a moor; for in such things we find it, give and receive it; but like manna it cannot be kept. At the time it seemed in no way strange to be so happy; and yet in retrospect I wonder how such riches could ever have been mine. I planted herbs at Gavin's door and tended the rose that grew against his wall; made him seats from the kipper-boxes cast up on the shore; left for him to find treasures thrown up by the sea, wave-worn wood, scallop-shells, cowries, mussel-pearls; and all his gifts to me were of the same kind, gifts beyond price. Such things were a language in which we communicated—or so I imagined, as I scattered everywhere what Blake calls the 'gold of Eden', hoping that he would gather it. Now I do not know if he ever found that fairy-gold, or if it turned

41

back, as such gold does, to a few withered leaves and worth-less pebbles and empty shells.

*

Because I was so happy to work at his table (I read Law's Boehme there, and Taylor's Plato, and worked on my Blake book, besides the poems I wrote) and to sleep under his roof and to tend his fire and to leave him treasures to find when he came and I left, I never doubted but he shared that felicity. 'Woman', Karen Blixen has written, 'as long as she is free to dwell in the thought of her love, even in the thought of an unhappy and hopeless love, has a home there. If the time ever comes when it is demanded of woman, as of man, that she must forget her love . . . then she will be driven out on the open, bleak field, without a shelter, exposed to the wind and the weather. Worse than that, she will be running like a mad creature, with dishevelled hair, mocking herself and her own nature.' My home was in my love; to Gavin's house, his earth and sky and sea and the fire on his hearth, I felt that I had come home. Was that so strange a happiness? It is not bodily presence but the presence to one another of two spirits which is the state of love, whether in physical presence or in physical absence. To be alone yet not lonely was to me a happiness I would not have exchanged. It was appropriate to me; for as a poet I inhabited a solitude, while as a woman I felt myself, in those days—and the days became years—invisibly companioned. 'Never again shall I be alone,' I thought; for a love which is rooted in holy ground, cannot fail. Gavin had himself once said of our relationship that it would be for all our lives. I thought, besides, that because I had re-entered Eden I must by mysteriously absolved; since how, but by divine permission, could I be there?

During those years I stayed at Sandaig in earliest spring before the snow had melted from the hills; in summer, in autumn: I would go during term, when my children were at school, whenever it so happened that Gavin was not himself there; and he was often abroad at the time. I seemed then to be not so much a person as an eye of the world, a pure consciousness in which the beautiful forms of creation were reflected. Again as at Martindale I could here forget myself, become, as it seemed, invisible, vanish into the elemental world and participate in its freedom and delight. It seemed not so much that Gavin and I were two people in one world, as that one world existed in our two minds, as if earth were a shared vision. So like was nature to imaginative vision that it seemed that Gavin and I had become dwellers in paradise, or paradise proved not, after all, to have vanished from the earth. For the experience was not other-worldly; it was, on the contrary, an epiphany of (so I still believe), the living essence of the natural world. I would sit long by the waterfall merely looking at the sunlight filtering through a green leaf, or bubbles forming and turning and drifting, or elvers ascending against the current; or listen to the wild voices of eider or plover or *ghilliebridhe*, or feel with my hand the warmth rising from an eider's nest, or breathe in the sweetness of birch or bog-myrtle, or taste the rain blowing in my face or the berries of the rowan. To perceive, to gather in that beauty, was to me like a task of love; it was as if a river were continually flowing between us, carrying to Gavin all I experienced. As if; for I no longer know whether this was so. But to me it was as if our consciousness were one and indivisible, and that consciousness the world we shared in the 'one mind'.

Certainly the experience owed nothing to whatever in me is peculiar to myself; to my by this time considerable knowledge in many fields, or such small command of language as the poet had by then acquired. Rather I seemed to have recovered a capacity to experience the world as Blake's 'one continued vision of imagination' which is perhaps the lost human norm, that from which we are fallen, a capacity we share with the animals, perhaps with the plants and the rocks themselves. I felt myself, then, to be one of the eyes of earth, Plato's 'happy immortal living creature'; and this knowledge immeasurably greater in

43

kind than any acquired knowledge of my individual experience. Of this I wrote in poems of the time; yet the poems captured, of all that vision, scarcely a glimpse or gleam, so continuous it was, and in itself such a happiness that even the desire to write often left me. There seemed, besides, to be plenty of time; for in the world of nature there is neither past nor future, nothing there has had a beginning nor will have an end; the eider seemed to have all the time in the world. All I saw proclaimed not transcience, but only 'the adorable I AM'. At once creator and creature of the vision it seemed enough merely to see and to live that world; the task assigned alike by love and the daimon of poetry.

I have at times believed, with the Neoplatonists, that the soul sheds its envelope of dust to emerge as moth from chrysalis; but there have been other times—and at Sandaig this was so—when it has seemed possible that what we call nature may prove to be a region of immortal spirit.

> Thought is its cradle and its grave, no less
> The future and the past are idle shadows
> Of thought's eternal flight. . . .

At best I saw so imperfectly, so inattentively, so never enough.

*

I thought to live in that world for ever; and allowed the days and weeks and months and years to pass. But nothing in time, permanent as the present always seems, shares the everlasting quality of those visions we so briefly glimpse between its moments. And I never noticed how, imperceptibly, the other kingdom was withdrawing itself as I grew to love too much those earthly forms in which, even so, it lingered for a very long time before the old story told itself anew; the woman's desire to possess what was given only to the poet; disobedience, anger, remorse, exile, the closed gates; I did not, after all, keep faith with the vision. If the 'one mind' remains for ever, I was not to remain for ever in it, as I had thought. As that mind brought Gavin and myself together, so now in that consciousness we were to be parted, as if by an invisible field of force which in my thoughts I could no longer cross.

For a time it must have given Gavin pleasure to have me in his house. And I believe that pleasure was the knowledge that I was working, upon his world, a kind of transmutation, through the alchemy of imagination. Mere gratitude for such small practical things as I had done for him cannot explain away this opening to me the doors of his world; and when I have heard that 'of course Gavin will always be grateful for the help you gave him by'—introducing him to so-and-so, some publisher, or whatever it was—I have the sense of a deeper betrayal than if I were to be told, 'Gavin hates you.' Yet it came to be as if I had never known Gavin, nor set foot in Sandaig. I could be easily persuaded that I never was there, that the poems I wrote were not mine; driven out of my own memories, 'driven out on the open, bleak field, without a shelter', that I myself had never existed. For those memories were Gavin's domain, and in recalling them I seem, now, to be trespassing in a place I have no right to enter.

*

How soon did mortality begin to creep in and to obscure an epiphany which, at the time and for long after, I had re-solved never to betray, never to fail? The first time Gavin's anger struck at the roots of my life we were on a journey together; he was on his way to Sandaig, and was to take me as far as Boothby, where I was to stay with Winifred Nichol-son. His racing-car had broken down near Stamford, which had delayed our journey by many hours; so that—a snow-storm meanwhile had come on—we had to stop for the night somewhere in the Pennines. I am tempted to say that I cannot now remember why we quarrelled; but I remember perfectly well: I had shown Gavin my diary; and such was his dismay that he lashed out at me in anger. To me that journal was a record of sacred things, a search for truth, the bearing witness to a vision. It was—I being a writer by habit my métier to write, and to forbid me to record my thoughts in words—and many of my thoughts concerned himself— must seem like forbidding me to live my life. To him, it was a woman's indiscretion, it was a potential danger, it was a threat to his reputation, a kind of potential blackmail. It was terrible to me to discover that he saw it so.

Years later, after a deeper estrangement, I was to watch all those diaries of Sandaig days turning and turning in the pool below the bridge at Lanercost, until the current caught them and carried them down the river Eden to be drowned somewhere in Solway mud. For long I had stood on that bridge, the parcel of books balanced on the parapet; unable to consign them to the river; for they were myself, a part of my life; it was a kind of suicide; and as I stood by that parapet I was in two minds as to whether to drown my books or myself. It was, in a way, a suicide; or a trial suicide, to see whether I could do it. It could scarcely have cost me more to destroy myself than to destroy for ever the record of my happy years. When the books were caught at last by the current I followed them downstream, watching them until they sank, as the river flowed through pastures towards the summer sunset.

The rift that opened then between us was, I now realize, profound; for me, all life is the raw material of poetry; for him, to write about another person is a betrayal of trust; a reasonable point of view; but one so remote from my own intentions towards Gavin—my love for him, my concern to do him only good—that his seeing me in the light of an injurer (or potential injurer) came as a shock whose violence seemed to tear my heart out by the roots.

That night, sleeping in a strange bed, at the heart of an unknown country of cold storm, I had a dream. I was walking down the familiar path to Sandaig; and when I had crossed the burn I could reach neither the house nor the tree, because a high palisade of wooden palings had been

46

built, ugly and hostile, and the beauty of the place all destroyed. The wooden barricade was a fit symbol of the wall built about the first Eden after the Fall; but—so mysteriously does the outer world mirror inner events—in the end, such a wooden palisade, precisely like the one in my dream, was (through logical sequence of events neither of us could then have foreseen) built; and I could never again return, and the place as I had known it was laid waste. A strange blending of symbolism and precognition; for symbolism might explain the barrier, but only precognition, surely, its precise form, those vertical wooden palings. But then, events of mind will always evolve event in the world; Macbeth's phantom dagger became a real dagger all too soon. We are both the creators and evolvers of our fate. Not only in our conscious acts, but also, above all, in our thoughts and passions, we create the events, though its form we cannot foresee. How uselessly we plead that we did not deserve that this or that should happen; for all that happens, good or bad, is but an enactment of our own deepest reality, a reflection in outer events of the inner pattern.

*

It is easy to see why, as a poet concerned only with perfection and habitually selecting images and symbols of ordered beauty, I disregarded as non-existent, unimportant, not to the purpose, the imperfect, the distorted, the vulgar, all which falls short and does not bear the stamp and signature for which I looked. That is not to say I do not see such things—on the contrary, I am jarred, bored, or pained as the case may be; but pay only so much attention to such things as is necessary for the putting of them from my mind. My own failures, or actions of which I am ashamed, I also long regarded as irrelevances, as fallings-short; my attention has never been held, like a certain kind of moralist, by evil either in others or in myself. My attention wanders from evil, in a kind of disdain to notice its essentially vulgar and worthless presence. For myself, spiritual effort has lain in

47

the effort to create, or merely to contemplate, some perfection, and has never taken the form of moral self-search-
ings, battlings with 'temptation' and the like. I think it is
true that in my friends I am interested only in what is good
in them, whatever it may be, disregarding the rest as irrel-
evant and not worthy of notice, as failures in them to be
what they really are. So we read those poems in which a
poet has succeeded in attaining some intended perfection,
and not those in which he has failed to do so; to do otherwise would be ridiculous. I have always looked for whatever
is best in people not from blindness to flaws and faults
(these are self-evident) but because I regard all that baseness
which the brilliance of Ivy Compton Burnett and her many
less talented analogues exposes as 'the truth' as, precisely,
its absence.

No doubt it is true that I have too much discounted the
negative power of evil both in myself and in others. Of this
Canetti warned me at the very outset of my relationship
with Gavin. He warned me that I was disregarding too much
other aspects of Gavin's character than those I chose to see.
I replied, with truth, that I saw Gavin's faults and shortcomings with perfect clarity, but that these had not a reality
comparable with the living essence I had also seen; with
deeper insight, so I believed; and since that essential beauty
is higher on the scale of reality than any shortcomings, so
it must also prevail. *Magna est veritas et praevalebit*: there is
nothing higher than the truth. Neither Loyola nor Plotinus
meant Ivy Compton Burnett's 'truth', nor the 'truth' of
this decade that holds the lowest and worst to be discovered
about any human being to be the 'truth', outweighing
whatever good they may have done, aspiration they may
have followed. Plotinus' truth these would call falsehood;
as he would have called their truth, the unreal. Therefore
I believed 'the real' Gavin to be that 'man of light' I had at
certain moments beheld, and not the mire and clay which
obscure the incorruptible gold of the soul. I argued that,
since Gavin had been brought to me by that immortal
48

world, he was the task assigned me; and that, with the help of those powers who had brought him to my door, I could not fail. I did not doubt that with such help I could, if need were, rescue Gavin from the abyss; such was my phrase; and I remember Canetti's words, spoken most gravely outside 9 Paultons Square, as he was taking leave of me at my door, 'Gavin for you *is* the abyss.'

Of course the evil I could not see was above all in myself. And it is also true that while I was willing and happy to accept my relationship with Gavin as a Platonic love, I never really at heart accepted his homosexuality. Perhaps I was not so naïve as to suppose that I could physically change him; yet I did think that on another level I could win his love. Was I too much my father's daughter, applying that puritan morality in which I had been brought up? Or was I, simply, too much a woman to accept what is 'against nature'? At heart I thought homosexuality to be wrong; though often enough excusable because of some early wound which had been its cause. Gavin had all my compassion. His mother, too, was a puritan; a devoted member of the 'Apostolic Church' founded by Irving (a friend of Jane Welsh Carlyle) of which her parents, the Duke and Duchess of Northumberland, had been prominent supporters, and the Maxwell family also. Had not a combination of family pride and puritanism too harshly restrained her much-loved youngest son; born, besides, after the death of his father, killed early in the first World War? At the dawn of adolescence he had, besides, suffered an illness so grave that his life had been despaired of; and so, thrown back into the power of his mother just at a time when he would naturally have been asserting his independence, was it not understandable that the real 'woman in his life' should be that mother, so devoted, so full of many admirable qualities? It was she who had taught him his love of poetry, encouraged his enthusiasms and protected his sanctuaries. So that other women, had, for him, become forbidden. That I could understand, for that I could feel compassion. Once he said

49

to me that he thought his mother could more easily accept that he had a homosexual relationship than a relationship with a married woman; 'or any woman', he sadly added.

But that homosexuality was either normal or good, that I could not accept. Insofar as I knew of such relationships I pulled against them. And I attributed to unquestionable morality an attitude that anyone but myself must surely have seen was vitiated by my own wish to possess Gavin for myself. He himself must have seen that very clearly. But I was so blinded by foolish pride in my renunciation of the flesh that I was blind to the emotional demands I made upon him.

I have always tended to like homosexual men, in part because of a certain 'feminine' sensibility of mind they so often possess; and Gavin did so beautifully possess that gift of compassionate understanding. 'I have not wisdom', he once said, 'but I have understanding.' He was a very humble person; and what he said was truly and humbly said. I also remember his quoting Traherne's words, 'No creature was ever loved too much, but some in a wrong way, and all in too short a measure.' Beautiful words. Gavin, unlike myself, was generous and humble in his love.

I had also liked the company of homosexual men because they made no physical demands upon me. I had been wounded in the sexual hunt when I was young and had by now become wary at evading any sexual approach. If a homosexual man likes the company of a woman it is for other (and better?) reasons. But with Gavin I was in love; another matter altogether.

Perhaps what Canetti meant was that although to me Gavin presented a sexless image, as if from that childhood where in truth we met, there was another side of his life that was not sexless. I saw him, perhaps, as I would have seen a priest, or a member of a religious order who had renounced the sexual nature; but of course that was not really the case. While I imagined a relationship transcending

50

the flesh, Gavin did not really believe in that kind of thing at all. On the one hand, physical attraction drew him elsewhere; on the other, he probably had grave doubts about my own motives. Was he right? Yes, and no. The poet was sincerely capable of Platonic love; and I believe that to that sincerity Gavin did respond. There was, after all, a bond between us. To the insincerity of the woman—the shadow the poet could not throw off—he responded differently; for that shadow was the devouring spider, the dark side of the woman, destructive, and the more dangerous for my unawareness of its presence.

Canetti had studied evil more closely than I; one might say he had specialized in it; he missed Vienna especially, so he used to say, because the English are 'not wicked enough', and this he found boring. When he warned me that Gavin was for me the abyss, and that I too much disregarded other aspects of his nature, he might have pointed out that the abyss opened also in myself, but he did not; and I was quite unaware of my own shortcomings at that time, as those who are filled with love are unaware of evil in themselves, since love intends none, intends such boundless good. We cannot ever measure that which we lack, wherein we fall short.

I have spoken of Canetti; and I cannot continue without at this point saying more about the friend to whom Gavin's brother first, I think (in affection and in only superficial irony), gave the name of 'the Master'. In the cafés where he sits (trying to recapture a lost Vienna) he is I believe known as 'the Professor'; though he is in fact one of the few among my friends who has at no time been involved with Academe. Both names are appropriate; which is not to say that the Master is infallible, or the Professor omniscient; he is indeed fated, like a character in one of his own novels, always to fail in his attempts to save from themselves those upon whom he expends so prodigally his intelligence, his compassion, his time; I am myself one of Canetti's failures. His novels, indeed, I find distasteful, for all their probing of the

51

mortal worms his characters are. Man is not, after all, a mortal worm, but an immortal soul, and to present humanity otherwise is to degrade, to caricature, to destroy the 'image of God' which the prophets of his own race beheld in us. Iris Murdoch put Canetti (or someone uncommonly like him) in one of her novels; a context not altogether inappropriate.

Canetti is quite possibly the most widely learned man I have ever met; perhaps he is the most intelligent. Yet it was neither for his learning, his intelligence nor his kindness that Socrates by his friends was called 'the best of men'. Perhaps the quality involved is wisdom; and Canetti's wisdom was of that specific kind Socrates claimed for himself: 'human wisdom'. Like Socrates Canetti is unimaginable away from the city; for him, as for Socrates, the human is his field of knowledge, the human experience at once his study and the medium of his creation. There are so-called 'humanitarians' who, filled with some Utopian dream, desire (like my father) to 'serve mankind'; but very few have any talent in the supreme art of the *comédie humaine*. Canetti has the genius of a Balzac for human beings; a genius which is at once a kind of intelligence and a kind of compassion, but is perhaps above all a love for the matter of his knowledge, as such. I am not alone in having felt that there is absolutely nothing of which I, in my highest or my lowest moments, might be capable of thinking or doing, that Canetti would not comprehend, imaginatively explore, make his own, know. There is a story (which profoundly shocked him, which surprised me, in view of his own low view of God) of Frederica Rose saying to Mme. Mayer, wife of the then French Cultural Attaché, 'Don't you think Canetti is exactly like God?'; to which Mme. Mayer replied, 'Yes, but is God like Canetti?' That remains, always, an anxious question; 'The son, how unlike the Father' Blake said, 'first God comes with a Thump on the head, and then the Son with balm to heal it.' So it is with Canetti, who, as a Jew, feels himself personally so to say responsible for that

52

'tiger-volcano', as I have heard him describe the god of the Jews, always ready to pounce or erupt. 'If I believed in one God, I should be obliged to hate him,' I have heard Canetti say; he is, however, a polytheist, whose pantheon is all the gods of the world, and more than have ever yet, or ever will be, known or named; in their multitude is his faith; in the inexhaustible and incredible riches of possibility, in whose grotesque improbabilities, self-contradictions, marvels and absurdities he delights. 'Behold Behemoth whom I have made'; what the God beyond reason revealed to Job in nature, Canetti beholds in that region of human thought in which abide the irrational forms of the gods. Unlike those psychologists who, blinkered by some theory or made impotent by 'detachment', or perhaps simply frightened by a world too full of things beyond reason, seek to reduce the teeming fertility of the imagination (or the Imagination) to some banality, Canetti lets things be. He would rather watch *supernatura supernaturans*, than relegate the supreme gods of all the ages from gold or stone to iron and the machine, to the ethnological section of any museum, or the files of case-histories. If there be insanity it is at large, and far exceeds the pathetic tentatives to be found in the wards of lunatic asylums. He loves the masks of the shape-shifters not for anything these might 'prove' to psychologist or theologian, but for their own sakes. What shocked him in the story I have told above was I suppose that he would not wish to be thought like the Jewish Tiger-volcano. (But to the second question, now, in 1976, I know the answer to be— No, God is not like Canetti. More, indeed, like Gavin, whose compassion and human understanding was not un-Christ-like; not, certainly proceeding from some high-place of intellectual pride that set him, in his own mind, above other poor suffering sinners.)

It was at one of William Empson's parties at Hampstead I first met Canetti; sometime during the war. I had never before seen anyone quite like him; as if tremendous energy had been compacted into his small but dynamic person. 'He is like a little lion,' that same Frederica said; but with all the energy of a large lion, or a whole pride of lions concentrated in his immense mental vitality. It was this vitality, coupled with an equally immense interest in people, which first impressed me in him; and no doubt I, like many others, found irresistible his evident interest in what I thought, did, was; an interest at once concerned and disinterested; for Canetti's concern (again like Socrates) is with the discovery and evocation of the essence of each person, with what Ibsen calls the vital illusion; only Canetti is not so cynical as to call anything which lives an illusion, seeing each as one more manifestation of the variousness of life. For those who want simple answers Canetti has none to give; he was essentially 'the Master' for those who wanted complex answers. Those who conversed with Socrates must all have left him not only with a clearer, but with an essentially more interesting notion of who and what they themselves were; and so it was with Canetti. Are we not most indebted to those masters who chip our statues out of our marble? So, as with Socrates, those who loved him did so principally for our own sakes, because he had the magical power of evoking from us, ourselves. Yet the converse is, perhaps, also true; as Gavin once said, 'none of us needs Canetti as much as Canetti needs us'. We were, indeed, his raw material, which every artist needs supremely; even though perhaps among his wide circle he has found some blocks of wood or stone or kinds of clay more to his purpose than others.

I had long thought of him as like Socrates in more essential respects before (I am reticent about even noticing people's physical appearance) I one day ventured to say to him (for the remark might not, after all, have been well received), 'Canetti, has anyone ever said that you look exactly like Socrates?' The Master, however, was already there: 'Yes, of course, it was my nick-name at school.' And to be sure he resembles exactly, as his loving and disrespectful disciples said of Socrates, one of those pottery figurines whose hollow interior is filled with little effigies of the gods. Balzac would have drawn from this physiognomical resemblance some long conclusion about the correlation of mental chracteristics with physical types: why was that wisest and best of men of an appearance which to the beauty-loving Greeks appeared ridiculous? And why do those who know Canetti best take more pleasure in his Socratic features, alive with intelligence and kindness, than in beauty itself? *Qu'est-ce qui est plus beau que la beauté*? To ask the question of Canetti is to ask it about the cosmos itself. I, by nature a Platonist, drawn to beauty and perfection, yet recognized in Canetti a principle beyond the beautiful; as in the sublime religion of the Jews I recognize a principle which transcends that of the Greeks. Beyond perfection itself there is marvel, there is inexhaustible possibility. 'The world is full of Gods' was said by a Greek, but could any Greek (for perfection tends to simplification and abstraction) have known how full? Would Socrates himself have tolerated even those neighbouring barbaric gods Aristophanes laughed at in *The Birds*? But Canetti delighted in the churinga stones of the Australian aborigines, fraught with the power of the ancestors; shape-shifters and devourers, maggot-gods, totems and demons. Yet in his room hung photographs of the sculptured saints of Chartres, and a post-card of Delphi showing that wisp of smoke which issues from its cleft in the rock as once from the Sibyl's cave; he would contain even the beautiful.

Once he said to me that it would be his wish, if that were possible, to experience the being of every creature in creation; for one whole day he said, he would like to be a worm—to know what it is to be that worm, so limited and inexpressive.

Loving in Canetti, as I did, a peculiar greatness, I was perhaps seeing in him an aspect of the race which was, and remains, in a special sense 'chosen' by that God of whom Canetti demands an answer to the predicament of his creature man beyond any the churches (including the synagogues) can give. Blake went to the heart of the matter, as always, when he saw that the god of the Jews, who spoke by the prophets and was incarnated in the Son of Man was the divine Imagination itself; and that therefore in time the whole world must come to 'worship the Jews' god'. If God chose to become incarnate in the Jewish race (as Christians are by their faith bound to believe) it was not, presumably, by one of those caprices which Canetti might attribute to the divine shape-shifter, but because of the natural aptness of the vehicle.

Other races have perhaps a greater metaphysical sense; Indians in particular. But in Canetti I recognized and valued a quality I have never found in even my perhaps more spiritually translucent Indian friends; that tendency implicit in the doctrine of the Incarnation of the Messiah, to a boundless concern for the weakest and the worst, a willingness to pay the ransom for the worm, which at the nadir of creation cries out to God to justify what there it must endure through its remoteness from the glory of a Heaven which is all wisdom and power. Defending God on one occasion I said that He did, after all, become Man in order to redeem man; and Canetti replied with unusual gravity, 'He could do no less.' To have taken on, as Canetti thinks he has done, the task of saving men from a relentless God is in the tradition of Abraham pleading for Sodom, of Ezekiel, or Jacob whose thigh-bone was dislocated in his struggle with the Most High; for if towards the rest of mankind Canetti had that compassion which he would feel towards the worm, upon himself he took divine responsibility. In this losing battle there was doubtless an immense pride, and yet he was within the tradition against whose God he so fought. Like the prophets before him he pleaded the cause of the worm before the Most High who created him, and whose sufferings, ignorance and, ultimately, his sins, must lie at the charge of his Creator.

If I noticed evil too little, Canetti explored its full extent, all its devious imaginings. At times he wearied of the task, like the god who 'repented him that he had made man';

wondering at times how much further down is the bottom to which he has taken upon himself to go?

As a prophet of the *nadir* he was a mind of his time. To Canetti there is nothing in the unfathomable stupidities of evil which he likes or admires; if he was concerned with the lowest places it was not, as with some of the literary company he may find there, as a propagandist for human vileness.

With Canetti I at times felt that the vision of the beautiful, of ideal perfection as the Greek philosophers have understood it, lacks some other quality without which all the outpoured abundance of the marvels would come to a standstill. Beauty has a marmoreal finality; if it be achieved, all ends there: is the lack we discover in perfection, imperfection? Creation is after all a flux away from, not towards, the still perfection of the One we call beauty, a fanning-out into a multiplicity of shapes and forms. The grotesque and the ugly are aspects of infinite possibility; and this too the Jewish genius has at all times best understood. We think of no single type of Jewish beauty, as we do of the Greek; rather the Jewish race runs to extremes, exemplifying, besides men and women of dazzling, almost excessive beauty, all manner of the grotesque and the ugly, and is not least within its genius (that genius being a fertile creative abundance of imagination) in the descending spirit which flows down into the lowest effects and into 'the many'; whereas the Greek genius tends always to ascend towards the highest causes, and towards 'the One' and 'the All', and the beauty of some norm.

Sitting with Canetti at the table of some shabby café open all night, he once remarked to me, I remember, that he came to such places 'to get clean', after any form of social pretence; finding in the shabby depths, among professional thieves and prostitutes, a kind of truth to the nature of things. The Greek philosophers call this world 'the dregs of the universe'; but just in those dregs the Jewish genius comes into its own; for it is to this point God must

57

descend if descend He will. Canetti at least would not spare Jehovah one atom of the mire and misery, the ignorance and depravity into which man, his creature, whom having made He must know is weak and foolish, has fallen. I remember how he pointed to the stains on the tablecloth between us, and said it was this, this with which he felt he must keep faith, which he must understand, towards which he was responsible; for in conversations with Canetti it is sometimes difficult to discover where he thinks his own responsibilities end, and those of the God whom he so relentlessly confronts with his evil deeds towards man, begins. Yet at times he has admitted that there may be 'the good God' somewhere beyond the cruel demiurge. Anyone who felt it necessary to define precisely Canetti's heresies would find abundance of material; but to argue whether he is right or wrong is a dead occupation; his own intense concern, comprehension, his genius for seeing into remote places of the soul's experience, and from points of view as strange as the eyes of bees or the tactile blindness of the Biblical worm, or Kafka's beetle, is more imaginatively revealing than anything that might be gained by placing him on a theologian's bed of Procrustes.

Canetti was not, however, without critics whose authority he himself acknowledged. Sometimes in his dreams, so he once told me, he would find himself in the presence of very old men, thousands of years old, far wiser than he himself; Chinese sages, perhaps, or simply sages. These very old men are to Canetti what Canetti himself was to those who thought of him as 'the Master': they laughed at him and his notions, and mocked him as a child.

'Christianity', I remember his once saying (very late at night when we had been talking for hours), 'is so vulgar;' I knew at the time what he meant, though I now find it difficult to put into words. He meant, amongst other things, that Christianity accepts with too easy a facility the answer to what seems to him God's worst outrage against man: death. To accept with facility, complacency, or sentimentality, the redemption of man from his mortal predicament, is to fail to confront the predicament itself. It is death, to Canetti, which is God's unforgivable crime against his creature man.

Sometimes it seems to me that there is something willed and put on about Canetti's way of seeing death, as of a false supposition followed up to see where it will lead. To the Platonist, the Buddhist or the Hindu death is nothing worse than the pain involved in dying (not so great, as a rule, as the pain involved in living) for the soul after death finds itself precisely where its actions have placed it, to reassume its task in this or some other world or situation; at worst to linger in those hells or purgatories of the soul which we travel here no less than there; and at best death is a homecoming of the soul to its own place. To the Christian death is more to be feared because it is believed that this one life determines for ever the situation of the soul in eternity. I myself greatly fear the Judgement (a reality understood alike by Christian, Platonist and Buddhist), the soul's confrontation with all that it most wishes to forget, the anamnesis of every shameful and cruel act, every betrayal of love, every baseness; everything I have forgotten because I dare not remember it; if I fear death it is not as extinction, but because it is not extinction. Death as such does not seem to me an ultimate issue at all; and even the Judgement is already present, here and now, and at moments we tremble before the silent reproach of the 'God within'.

Neither presumably can death seem an outrage to a simple-minded positivist; for if the soul be not immortal, there is no mystery in the dissolution of a creature who is, like the Archbishop of Canterbury in the primer of zoology, ninety-something percent water. Only from Canetti have I caught even a glimpse of what the issue at stake was, on the Cross: death as such. If the souls are immortal, as the Pythagoreans and the Indian metaphysicians believe, in what sense had man to be 'saved' from death, or death 'overcome'? If there be such a question, the answer to it (the answer imprinted on the Holy Shroud) could only have been found by a man of Canetti's race; not by a Father Pius, believing implicitly in the immortality of the soul, or any visionary who has gazed into the Christian heavens, or any heavens at all; for death is the tragedy specifically and only of earth, of the mortal worm, of the human condition as it is in this world. Therefore the question is not, for Canetti, to be evaded by the postulation of other worlds or other states of being; these may or may not be; but the mere fact of this world, of this state, that such a world can exist at all, anywhere in the universe, he sees as a reproach to to God so great that he cannot forgive the creator of mortal man who has to endure, in this world, his mortality. In what way can the heaven of heavens obliterate the reproach of the everlasting Belsen? Therefore if death is to be conquered it must be in this world, for the reality exists in no other.

'If I could really believe that Jesus had conquered death I would become a Christian tomorrow,' he once said; for what seems to him 'vulgar' in Christians is, precisely, their complacency, the facility with which they are willing to accept a promise so immense. If it were true that Jesus on the Cross conquered death, then, Canetti felt, all that human suffering, that innocent blood which beneath the altar of a relentless Creator cries out for vengeance, might be atoned for by the god who shed it; for it is not what man has done to God, but God to man, which seems to him to cry out for atonement.

In saying I really do believe the soul to be immortal (and not only on the testimony of Plato and Plotinus, but from such insights as have been mine) I have felt, in Canetti's presence, ashamed, because I have never, as he has, known or envisaged the darkness of the farthest places of the universe, into which (according to Islam) the Angel of Death, looking once on every day of Allah, asks, if God has created anywhere a world more terrible than this; not terrible because of rectifiable injustices, but as such. Such is the dark

60

reverse of the other truth, Plotinus' saying that no world could be more beautiful than this, except that Other.

I have, all in all, admired Canetti more unreservedly, taken more pleasure in the riches of his imagination, that inexhaustible robber's-den of treasures that reveals itself to those who possess the *open, sesame*, than in the mind of any other person I have known well; and yet I have adopted none of his ideas; on the contrary it would be hard to find anyone more naturally remote from his kind of thought, his way of experiencing, from his self-chosen vocation as the advocate of the mortal worm, than I am. I love the order of nature and shun the chaos of cities; I am always looking for a way out from what Canetti travels always more deeply into, the chaos and the ignorance of the human condition. I desire the perfection of eternity and the beauty of the gods; he, like a Boddhisattva, would not permit himself such a luxury as beatitude, or escape from the human condition before the last blade of grass has attained salvation; and if he has contempt for any human being, it is for those who would do so. In Canetti's presence I feel myself condemned as imperfect just because I have sought perfection. Only, I have come to realize, a Jew can really understand Christianity.

All the same (for after all, in my apologia I may surely speak for myself), I am too proud (and so, for that matter, is Canetti) to join the universal whine of the plebeian sense of grievance which blames God, the Government, the state of society, etc., etc., for the existence of suffering; or the plaint of self-pity which lays our unhappiness or failure to the charge of parents, marriage-partners and other people in general. I do not know what those mean who speak of 'rights' which are somehow due to us: have we any, within this mysterious universe? We are all, besides, very good at pitying the hypothetical and remote situations of others, even while knowing very well our own capacity to endure, when it comes to the point, whatever has to be endured. To suppose others lacking in this after all primary human quality seems to me to deny the mortal condition its single dignity—the human capacity to sustain it; not, after all, for very long.

*

'We met at last in the heart of an otter'; so he inscribed my copy of his first book, *Harpoon at a Venture*; the book I used to be called to listen to at all hours. He wrote the inscription in Italian; easier to say such things in a foreign language; for it was, in its way, perhaps, an admission of something which can only be described as love; if two things equal to the same thing (Mij's heart) are equal to one another.

For Mijbil was the bond that united us. 'May I be his godmother?' I had said to Gavin, as we sat, side by side, watching that enchanting living being swimming in my bath at No. 9 Paultons Square, where he had been brought to call on me. And so it was.

Gavin had brought Mij back from an expedition to one of the four legendary rivers of Paradise (the Euphrates); it is all told in *Ring of Bright Water*. But what he did not tell—at my own wish did not tell—was that whenever he went away for a time he would leave his otter cub in my care, sometimes in London, sometimes at Sandaig; and Mijbil was attached to us equally and alike. It may sometimes be that the love of animals is a substitute for some human love; but for us it was precisely its not being human which made this bond so magical. In the heart of this creature we both loved, warm with the one life-blood of the earth, Gavin and I were united indeed. Mij was a gate-keeper who allowed us to pass, through his life, into the unfallen world of those who there play in the everlasting play of life without guilt or sorrow. It was as if we had been released from our fallen humanity and allowed to return among those still innocent children of paradise.

Not only to love nature but to be loved by nature; to understand the language of the birds, the wordless language of animals. It was given us to enter the fragile essential life sheltered within that warm sleep of an animal curled up, making of itself the closed circle of a microcosm, and at the invisible centre of the body which so precariously guards and shelters it, a spark of immemorial life, a star of life that has travelled in unbroken succession from the beginning, the source. By the protecting, the preserving grace of nature, there it sleeps, black nose hidden in warmth of fur, all the delicate senses sealed in a magical sleep as secure as the circulation of the stars in the night-sky; a darkness no less spacious and still than that into which sleeping life withdraws. On my bed he slept, secure and fragrant, entrusting to me his sleep in the sympathy of that one life we shared; his paws encircling my ankle, or his breathing mound fitted to my shape. On barren rock by barren sea that living creature has lain curled on my knee asleep, microcosm warm with life and warm in the sun, marvel of the animal, so vulnerable to the pounding of water, the cold of wind and rain, the destructive teeth of rock; breathing the violent air so softly in and out of its small lungs; an organism so complex, so vulnerable, raising into existence, at the heart of that desert of rock and wind and water, a consciousness so delicate, so boundless a joy.

Through that magical participation Gavin and I entered the world of the animal itself; for it was not in our world, not a domesticated pet, but wild and free. Each morning he woke into his joy, bounding over the grass to dive and play in the reaches of the burn, calling me to follow, to share his delight in the little fish he found under stones and ate alive with such simplicity of innocence; his delight as he dried his coat in the hot sand. To me he would come bounding, streaming with salt water, to wreathe himself round my neck, whistling with joy and summoning me to join him in that unending play; tugging at the corner of my coat with his teeth to make me follow him into those lovely pools. Up the stream I would follow him, or round the shore; and always he would rejoin me, racing back to me in a rapture of re-union that was always new. He did not obey me; rather the reverse, it was I who followed his wild pleasure into a world where there was always time enough; or no time at all, for every moment was a present without beginning or end.

The only bond between us was love; I was bitten once or twice, and carry those little white scars as the only evidence I ever walked in that unfallen world with Gavin's animal-angel. I did not seek to impose any human obedience upon his wildness; but we had charmed one another into a devotion that was a tie, as I thought, more secure.

Such was my precarious happiness; for if our loving animal belonged, properly speaking, to Gavin, in Mij's unawareness of such a distinction I forgot that he was not mine too. Once I remember Gavin arriving at Sandaig to take over his domain and his water-baby from me; we were by the burn; and Mij bounded first to his master, then to me, racing back and forth, sharing an equal allegiance, in a wild, unbounded joy.

*

Out of what far-back roots, then, did the destructive forces grow? Resentment and pride, where did they begin? Far back, all through my life, acts of cruelty, ruthless in-difference, neglect, wilfulness, blindness; all these had made me what I now was; and from what I was, not from what I intended, came the consequences. Of course Gavin also had faults and behaved very badly towards me in many ways (I have now forgotten in what ways, but at the time he caused me much suffering, which was not, presumably, all my fault). For if the world of the Logos, of the imagination, is our meeting-place, its landscape that native country of which all poetry tells, its life the one love all creatures give and receive, our human selves are peculiar to ourselves, each a different lonely prison-cell, alike only in limitation, imperfection, in being cut off and solitary. We do not know what goes on in others' lives immediately by participation (as in the world of imagination) but by guess and deduction,

64

often false. Pride, Gavin said, was my especial fault; and through a perfectionism more Platonic than Christian, I lacked, perhaps, compassion for the prisoners in the prison-cells; while he, more Freudian than Platonist, seemed to me often not to understand the value of pearls, taking them for diseased acorns. At all events he often turned and rent me; or so it seemed to me. But I do not know how it seemed to Gavin—how Gavin saw me; for that is the one thing no person can know of another, once we stray outside that self-forgetful love that never asks such things, or doubts that self-delighting life is lovable. So it was with our loving otter, so it is with little children. Being what I was, I think I could not have loved Gavin more; but the love of an imperfect fallen creature, to what does that amount? My unbounded sense of giving blinded me to the truth that, giving ourselves, we give the bad with the good.

Self-accusation is too facile a kind of truth-telling, only one degree less false than the first instinctive response of our natural humanity, the blaming of the other person the world at large and even (*pace* Canetti) 'God'. For all the time we were, Gavin and I alike (as all are), standing our judgement in the light of the world we had each momentarily glimpsed. Of this I was—I cannot in false humility deny even now—mindful at all times; of my vow of obedience to that vision to which I remained, to the end, oriented even when only to know myself thereby condemned. I was (to speak now of the heart of love, which lies beyond the frontiers of egoism) prepared to do and suffer anything and everything for Gavin's sake; I felt my love to be a kind of Atlas upholding the heavens and in this arduous interior labour I felt myself privileged, dedicated, blessed. Whatever Gavin asked of me I did; he was at all times in my thoughts and in my prayers. Afterwards people would say—even Gavin's mother, and his brother, 'Kathleen helped him, she introduced him to X and Y,' who found him a publisher, or reviewed his first book favourably or some such negligible thing; Gavin himself might later have said so, thereby

65

putting our relationship into a category of an external kind. I have 'helped' many people in that kind of way, but to Gavin I gave not 'help' but something infinitely more dangerous and incalculable, myself.

Unfortunately it is in virtues and good intentions that egoism most securely entrenches itself; we like to see ourselves in a good light, and in our ostensible good-doing self-criticism is silenced. Having thought—perhaps truly—that Gavin had been brought to my door by divine providence in order that I should help to draw him up out of the complex troubles into which he, a companion so dear, had fallen, I did not notice where selfless instrumentality ended and egoism began; when I ceased to be the agent of the 'one consciousness' and became mere woman, trying to purchase a continuance of Gavin's affection by loading him with superfluous benefactions, in order to extort from him gratitude. Imperceptibly our roles were reversed; it was no longer he who needed me, but I who needed him; I could no longer contemplate my life without Gavin, nor did it occur to me that Gavin might feel otherwise. For in that other kingdom love is given and received; there is no thought of 'possessiveness' and the like except where there is no longer any love. I cannot even imagine, now, what my supposed benefactions were, when I was in fact his debtor, he having opened to me his world, lent me his house, allowed me to participate in the love of his so much loved Mijbil bestowed on me the lost domain of paradise. But I felt myself the giver because I loved him, and love's desire to give and illusion of giving is boundless.

In the two kingdoms there are two realities, and these seldom at one. Whereas I continued to remember the world which had brought us together, Gavin, I began obscurely to realize, no longer saw in me anything but my shabby human self.

To my own shabby exterior, my bodily appearance, my human personality, such as it is, that bearer of daimonic burdens, I had never throughout my life given much

66

thought; knowing myself only as an invisible consciousness; surprised and even resentful when I have seen a photograph of myself, so little has the person who can be photographed seemed related to that invisible self. I have always imagined myself as coming and going unseen in the world, feeling a shock of surprise, indeed of panic, when I am told I have been 'seen' in some place by some person of whose presence I was not aware. There is something deeply disquieting in the knowledge that we are at all times involuntarily present and visible. Perhaps I have been unwise so to disregard the shadowy image for which I am, after all, responsible, since it is I who cast it. I might have understood, had I looked at that shadow, how I must have appeared to Gavin; and to his mother, who saw in me the granddaughter of the Kielder schoolmaster, a divorced woman, an associate not to be desired for her son. But I thought Gavin had seen my invisible self, the poet, the chosen one of the daimon.

As I began more and more to sense that in Gavin's eyes I was of little worth, the being who wears me like a shabby disguise made no protest, though she saw, and suffered; for we cannot make ourselves known unless the eye of love can discern that hidden being we each of us are. I had thought Gavin had seen in me, as I had seen in him 'the face I had before the world was made'; now my disquiet came from the sense of some incalculable misunderstanding; and if my tears were one part mortal, they came, too, from the grief of the imagination at the betrayal of the immortal. Perhaps the truth was too simple for me to realize; as Canetti once said to me (I did not believe him) 'You must understand, Kathleen, that Gavin does not love you.'

But that was to me inconceivable. Love has a meaning, a reality; but to not love is, in 'the kingdom not of this world', something without meaning, unimaginable. Yet I was aware of a growing sense of cross-purposes; which, since I was at that time incapable of realizing Canetti's simple fact, 'Gavin does not love you,' seemed to me a betrayal by Gavin of a sacred bond. I was willing to do anything for Gavin in the name of that bond, but increasingly I felt that I was being made use of for trivial ends. My pride, certainly, was not that of the woman. Just because the woman seemed to me instrumental, I felt nothing to be beneath her; the woman did not stand on her dignity (upon what dignity could she have stood?) but because I regarded myself as instrumental I was not prepared to find that Gavin regarded the slave of the lamp as an ordinary slave.

But I sensed more and more that in Gavin's eyes I was only my mortal self. 'Poor old Kathleen, you look like a fat squaw', he once said to me, when he had reduced me to tears. I did not even feel this as an insult; the poet in me was too proud, the woman too unconcerned, for the shaft to wound me; but I did mind for Gavin's sake, and my grief was for him, for what seemed to me his inability to see any longer the fairy-gold I offered. So, bewildered, I endured much silent grief; and the sea within, the sea from which that visionary blossoming tree had arisen, at first blue as heaven, became yellow and green, then purple and black, and the water began to seethe below.

*

So far I had written. Now on this January morning of 1976, I write in my own hide-away cottage in Cumberland; not many miles from Bavington across the Northumbrian border; nor many miles from my mother's birthplace (Longtown) nor from Kielder, where the lives of our parents and grandparents crossed so long ago. In spring and autumn I see the grey-lag geese fly towards the sun setting over the Solway, and Gavin's childhood home. Can I be more truthful now? Do I know more of 'the truth?' For, as Gavin once said, there is no such thing as 'the truth'; only a different story, experienced by each of the participators. But if I tell my truth, I must include in it a confession of my culpable disregard of Gavin's point of view. If I felt, as oftener and oftener I did feel, aggrieved and resentful towards Gavin, this was on no better grounds, as it now seems to me, than that I suffered. Because I suffered I supposed that he had hurt me. That is an instinctive reaction, but both stupid and unjust; for most often we hurt ourselves, whether by imagining non-existent wrongs, or in persistence in some mistake we cannot or will not see. I can no longer even remember what my supposed grievances were or why I suffered; I can remember the stab of suffering well enough, that seemed like a dagger in my solar plexus often for days or weeks on end; but when I ask myself, what did Gavin do to cause that pain, I am compelled to admit that I can't remember that he did anything at all. I think I lost Gavin's affection not through his breaking faith, but through my own. If I had remained the poet, if I had not slipped so imperceptibly into demanding emotionality, he would not have broken faith with me. I became the spider, and he knew it.

It would be all too easy to say that Gavin's homosexuality lay between us; yet I do not think this need have been so but for my emotional possessiveness, and but for my continuous silent disapproval of his homosexual relationships. And I doubt whether any woman can ever feel otherwise, however much we may make an effort, on principle, to do so. Yet I was content to believe myself 'the woman in his life'; bewildered as I was, once, when he escorted Princess Margaret on a few occasions I told myself that this might well have been in order to please or simply to impress his mother, who would have seen such a match as altogether appropriate for her son, as, of course, in respect of birth it would have been. But I did not take the episode seriously, and it was, besides, very brief.

Then, again, there had been an evening when I fled from Gavin's studio on finding there a pair of gloves left, as he said, the previous evening by a woman friend he had met through me—a slight acquaintance of mine. My flight, unreasonable and instinctive, was an act of what must have seemed to Gavin emotional possessiveness. Yet I would not have felt this had the gloves been (say) Janet Adam Smith's (whom he also met through me) and later events proved my instinct correct. When soon afterwards Gavin took the owner of the gloves to stay with his brother at Monrieth, I felt both hurt and slighted. My Achilles' heel of vulnerability was Ilford; and whereas the poet is classless, I had a momentary clear realization that to Gavin and his family I was, poet or no poet, Ilford; and not socially acceptable in their own world. There I think I was unjust to Gavin who did respect the poet when I *was* the poet; and if I insisted on playing the woman, that was my fault. Again, the handsome friend he took to Monrieth was far more 'permissive' than I in the matter of his homosexual relations. Very much so, indeed.

In the event she became for a short time engaged to his brother; and once again my fears subsided, and I was only too glad to tell myself that they had been unfounded.

However, Gavin's possible social estimate of me troubled me the less because my own circle of friends were, after all, in their own right, distinguished. Helen Sutherland, whose house had become to me a second home, judged on a different scale. Gavin's painting she would not have taken seriously at all; his books she might have read; but as light reading, not as she read David Jones, or Eliot, or Herbert Read, or even as she read my own poems. To her Gavin and his world would have appeared philistine; though she did think Gavin charming: 'like a sword—or a lily', was her phrase; 'a fleur-de-lys'. So that while Gavin may have held social reservations about myself, I, by other standards, had similar reservations about him. Every art or science has its own standards of excellence and its own aristocracy. That, after all, is what aristocracy, for Plato, is. And that, surely, was why Gavin and I could meet on equal terms at all. He respected my values, when I lived by them; and I his, for I saw in his freedom, his disregard of cautious self-interest and all practical obstacles when there was an adventure in question, something that characterizes a hereditary aristocracy, and is in itself admirable, and without which the world is likely to be the poorer. Truth to say neither Gavin nor I acted from self-interest of that kind in matters that concerned our self-appointed tasks. Both of us alike knew what Conrad calls 'the unknown discipline of the self-imposed task'.

Gavin had another quality which likewise he owed, no doubt, to his birth: he had the gift of making us all his slaves. It came naturally to Gavin to initiate adventure, and to assign the parts to those who gladly joined him. He had also—less admirable—a way as I think all his friends would agree—it was perhaps quite unconscious—of confiding in each of us as though we alone were the one confidante, the one friend upon whom he could rely, to whom he could turn for help. He would summon me at all kinds of times—I must go round now, at once, to resolve some crisis, to advise him on what he was writing or on some other matter; and, of course, I always went, happy to be asked, to be needed; as women always are when we love. Gavin avoided the social scene, he was happiest in these intimate meetings, preferring, too, his own surroundings to going out; although he did often come to me, saying that in my room he found an atmosphere of peace always. Only long after did I realize to how many others he had behaved just so; and they too doubtless were misled, as I was, into believing that they alone were needed. If misled is the right word.

So, with or without reason, I suffered. How vulnerable we are when it is we who love; indeed to love is to allow ourselves to be vulnerable. How heartless we are to those who love us! I do not mean sexual love, for I am inclined to think that, in matters of sex all's fair, whatever may be the case in war. The raw instinct has its own laws which are those in 'nature'. I think I suffered, when I was young, too many scruples in the matter of sex, and God knows too few in the far more humanly significant matter of love. I think, now, of my mother, whose boundless love for me over all these years I had called 'emotional possessiveness'

71

and closed myself against as if it would destroy me. Yet now, myself the lover against whose emotional possessiveness Gavin had perhaps closed himself in a like fear, I knew how little, really, love asks; just that the other person should be open to us, should receive the love we give. Then, the demon-face they fear would be transformed to beauty. If I had only received and valued my mother's love, how little she would have asked; and was not I the loser who for long years kept her at a distance, offering her, as now I began to feel that Gavin offered me, only the exterior self? I hated and feared her tears, that I could so easily have wiped away. There is a law in these things and was I not now reaping what I had myself sown? Now it was I whose love was met with something that was not love. Whatever God may be— the 'one consciousness', the law of Karma, the ground of reality in which we live, move and have our being, that reality is not mocked, the law is both just and inexorable. All our debts must be paid.

Only once did I pass a night with Gavin. He had been desperately wretched and asked me if I would so stay; on the understanding, of course, that there should be no sexual contact between us. And to that I gladly agreed. Yet to me that act was binding as no marriage had ever bound me. When we remove our clothes we remove, as it were, an armour, a disguise. The poor physical body, so defenceless, so vulnerable in its nakedness, can communicate more than any words. We come from the womb, the breast that com- forts us is mortal flesh. But how could Gavin, who must have shared his bed with so many, have imagined that to me, twice married and with two children, that simple act was total commitment? Every night of my life, since then, I have spent alone. This has troubled me but little for, increasingly of late years, I have come to realize that we are always, at all times and places, in the total embrace of God. Whoever knows this is never lonely.

At last, one evening at Sandaig, the storm broke. I had been staying at Sandaig, as usual, with Mij; and Gavin was to come, that day, to take over from me. I was about to leave our paradise where for so many weeks I had wandered by the shore and up the burn with our beloved otter. Like some shrine I had tended Gavin's house, happy to be there and to scatter, as I thought, fairy-gold for him to find; shells, and stones from the shore, things I had made or done for him. I was to sleep, that last night, at Mary and John-Donald's cottage, as usual; Gavin was bringing a friend with him.

I do not know whether, then, in feeling myself unwanted when Gavin came I reacted to his real thoughts; I would like to believe I misconstrued them. But the sense of some invisible, intangible outrage not so much against myself as against that of which I had thought myself the guardian, seemed as clear as a scene momentarily lit by lightning. All that intangible web of love I had woven I felt was brushed aside as if it was nothing to him.

For whatever reason, or unreason, I left the house in all the anguish of my real or imagined rejection, and went to the rowan-tree we both loved; the tree I had freed from the tangle of old wire that had cut into its bark, the tree where I had thought 'here and now I am in the place on earth I would most wish to be'. Weeping I laid my hands upon the trunk, calling upon the tree for justice: 'Let Gavin suffer, in this place, as I am suffering now.' I was at that moment beside myself, as one-pointed and as blazingly clear as a streak of lightning as I spoke aloud my terrible invocation. And I went up the hill to Mary and John-Donald with the dagger of anguish turning in my heart.

Two days later my white-hot grief had died down; but the anger and anguish I then had felt had risen from the depths. No less than the vision of the Tree in its living beauty, those words came from beyond myself. Happy are those who do not understand the power of thought to accomplish events.

It is said that a curse always recoils upon the person who utters it; and mine was to take full effect, both upon Gavin and upon myself. Such an invocation cannot be revoked by the mere recovery of temper and good-will towards the person against whom it is uttered. It has a life of its own; when a passion is so powerful as to stir those depths, we awaken forces beyond human control. But for a year all went on outwardly as before; Gavin leaving Mij in my care, as always, when he was away or abroad. He never knew of my invocation of the hidden lightning, and I thought the curse had died with my anger.

*

Easter came round, and again I was to take Mijbil to Sandaig. All seemed peaceful and my anger forgotten, yet on the day before I left London Gavin had spoken some words that had stirred my sleeping resentment; and again I cannot recall what cause I had, or thought I had, to feel again that anguished sense of inner betrayal. Perhaps I had none; that only he can ever know. But again it passed; I was only too willing to think I had been wrong. When I stepped out of Bruce Watt's boat onto that well-loved strand, that joyful otter-cub tugging at my wrist in the delight of his return to freedom, never had Sandaig seemed more beautiful, never had I felt more deeply the sense of home-coming. Never had I come with a more profound resolve to do all well, all right.

I had for a long time been writing no poetry; for my poetry had come to depend upon Gavin, upon some word that I wanted him to speak. But the word had not been said, and the springs were frozen. Now I had begun to wonder if perhaps my relationship with Gavin depended, rather, on the poetry than the poetry upon that relationship; if perhaps I, closing the gates of my injured heart against my daimon, and refusing to write, were to blame; seeking to force from Gavin the word love would not speak, for poetry's sake; for I knew that, little enough as Gavin might care for me, he cared a little for my poetry. But now I had made one of my periodic resolutions to seek again the threshold of the gods within if purity of intention could

74

raise me there. I knew that, for me, poetry is my only way to travel that spiritual journey; and my poetry has at all times been the expression of such intuitions as have come to me from that world. All other ways and means have, I have always known, been evasions of my task; and attempts to follow techniques of meditation and the like I have always in the end been forced to admit were make-believe. Nevertheless I had, besides intending to write poetry, asked an Indian friend to give me a *mantram*; and each day I rose in the morning and for an hour walked with my animal companion by the burn or on the strand, my will turned towards that steep ascent to whose foothills I thought I had at last come with the intention of never turning back. Never had I been so happy; never had my joyous companion been so happy; every hour of every day was filled with beauty; and I did not guess that these days of such strange exalted happiness were to be my last. I invoked the spiritual world, repeating aloud my *mantram*, and thought by so doing to call down only good upon Gavin, upon my own work, and upon the living creature whose love united us; for I could not imagine any good in which Gavin and I were not in harmony. I asked at the tree that my anger should be forgotten; and in the joy of my magical companionship, and all the poignant beauty of early spring, the scent of the young birch-leaves while there is still melting snow in the air; primrose and anemone and golden saxifrage, the green linnet singing on the budding alder, it seemed that innocence and beauty outweighed all evil.

But for all the radiance that streamed continually from the world within and behind nature, there was a continual undercurrent of anxiety, a daily realization of the hazards of a relationship with a young animal essentially wild, bound to me by bonds only of love. For he could climb cliffs where I could not; bound up the wet precarious stone ledges behind the waterfall where I could not follow; swim round rocky headlands at high tide, that I could not pass; nor would he always answer my call. There were alternations of wildness, which called him away; and love, which drew him back: he was not subject to human will. There were times when I scrambled up cliffs to meet at the summit my loving animal bounding to meet me with all the delight of re-union after separation, to follow me home at my heels like a dog. There were days when I would follow wet foot-marks on the dry stones up the burn, only to lose the track at last and return home in desperation, to find a breathing mound curled up on my bed, under the blanket. Worst of all were the times when he would swim round the headland; then I would follow in a little rowing-boat, coasting the rocks where the beautiful weed and anemones and sea-urchins grow, the sea-garden where he loved to play; watching for his little black head to break the surface of the water, and calling and calling. Most often I returned alone; and once he stayed away all night, and all the neighbour-hood was aroused to watch for him; news came that he had been seen, more than a mile down the coast; but when I went rowing round by the loch and calling, he was not there; but, again, there was the joy of returning to hear his whistle of welcome as I entered the house all but desperate. He always came back of his own accord; would always have come back.

Yet there were so many dangers to threaten his life. He had a little harness, and a lead could be attached—very necessary in London, or in travelling. Gavin told me it was unwise, even at Sandaig, to let him run without his harness. But I thought I knew better, imagining every possible accident: what if his harness should be caught in some snag? Some tangle of wire? Worst of all, what if this were to happen under water and he be drowned? When he was lost I would imagine him thus trapped somewhere, unable to return. This had happened more than once when he was with Gavin and he had returned with the harness broken, after some long struggle to free himself. I disobeyed and allowed him to run without his harness; I thought it was safer so.

Another instruction Gavin had given: he could be taken

south, down the shore, but it was unsafe to take him north, for in that direction lay the nearest village, and danger. Again, I thought I knew better. Day after day I took him south; but what was the way of that perilous headland where at high tide he used to disappear, leaving me helpless to follow; and of that cliff where I so perilously had climbed after him; and in this too I disobeyed Gavin. Knowingly I disobeyed; I thought I knew best; I forgot that the responsibility lay, finally, with Gavin, forgetting that the little animal who loved me, and whom I loved, was not mine, nor Sandaig, nor all that world to which my love was so wholly and irrevocably given. Love does not think in such terms; if these belonged to Gavin, so did I. I had nothing that was not his, not even my poetry, for that too came from the ground upon which we were, as I believed, as one.

I say that I acted as I thought best; but again I must be truthful: again some small thing in a letter had wounded me, and stirred that sleeping interior sea. Was it, in part, this pain of resentment which inclined me, in the last days at Sandaig, to disobey Gavin? Step by step, not realizing what I did even while I did it, I myself became the agent of the vengeance I had invoked.

More and more, each day of that last month of lovely spring, I realized the danger. Sometimes it seemed an open secret between Mijbil and myself; as if he was, or I was, fey; and I would talk to him, begging him not to find his death. Sometimes I prayed that he might at all events remain safe, until I could hand over my charge to Gavin. I seemed to know that his life was every moment hanging on a thread But where I ought to have obeyed Gavin and put on his harness, I relied upon prayer; I could not believe that the daimons and the elementals, the guardians and the invisible agencies of the world behind the world, of which all this seemed an embodiment, would fail me, if with them I kept faith.

Even so there was an evening—three days before Gavin was to come—when I even got out the harness, intending to

77

put it on; but it was so difficult to put a harness on that slippery limber form, and one was liable to get bitten in the process; so I deferred it.

Next day, at the time of our evening walk, the tide was in; and I feared to risk again that headland where so often before my charge had eluded me; and when we came to the mouth of the burn, I remembered Gavin's instructions, never to turn north; instructions I had hitherto strictly obeyed. But now I argued with myself that to do so was safer than the risk of losing my animal at the point, at high-tide. I disobeyed Gavin and turned north. And in that direction I saw growing, no doubt from some packet of bulbs washed up on that desert shore from a passing boat, a many-headed clump of golden narcissi; but their warning I did not heed: like Persephone those golden flowers lured me in the forbidden and fateful way.

After a few wild joyous comings and goings my animal companion swam out to sea, suddenly wild, and deaf to my call; and he eluded me. The animal-soul of our strange, magical, but doomed relationship swam away for the last time. At its appointed hour—and how far back, in the origins, was that hour appointed—for all my prayer, my love, my desperate desire to avert and avoid disaster, the lightning struck; and Gavin, through my thought and through my deed, though against my conscious will and knowledge, suffered at my hands the worst bereavement it was possible for him to suffer; a lonely man, his love was all given to his little otter. To Gavin and to me, he was more than an animal; a creature of paradise, a part of ourselves. In him I loved Gavin; in his love, a part of Gavin loved me, and Gavin through him accepted a part of my love.

What consolation could it be to either of us that I suffered no less than Gavin? For besides grief I must endure remorse.

That night I did not sleep; I hoped against hope that in the morning I would hear Mij whistling again at the door, left open for him. I lay in anguish, listening to a storm the like of which I seemed never before to have heard, the wind full

78

of lamenting voices as the ragged cloud flew over the moon from the south-west as the gale raged. Anger and grief were in the wind; and though I did not yet know it, all was over, Eden lost, its gates closed against me for ever. With sick hope I awaited the dull morning of the day, and renewed my fruitless search; and at last I heard that an otter had been killed by a workman on the road; yet even then it seemed impossible, unimaginable; it might have been some other otter; I watched the sea still for that little black head, long after I knew.

It seemed incredible that he should have gone, should be dead, not for that day only, but for the next and the next, and all possible days; that there should not be, in all the future, a day to hope for, when he would return. I have much fortitude, and have spent months and years of my life waiting and hoping; never before had I been compelled to forgo hope. But why say more? That finality of death needs no telling of mine. But mourning at last may find comfort in the very love that is its source; remorse never.

I had looked forward with so much joy to the day of Gavin's arrival that, all that cold empty day, there was in my mind a double image, as on a photographic plate: of the reunion I had hoped for, of Gavin and our loving otter; I had pictured the wild loving joy and the laughter of that reunion; and the many things I would have to tell, of the comings and goings and doings, of the anxieties and the happy returns of my animal companion, restored again to Gavin with the addition of so much of my love as he could be the bearer of. And another image, still unfamiliar, strange and blank in its features, not yet lived-with like the image of joy that had accompanied me on all those mornings and evenings up and down the burn and across the strand and by the rocky shore. Death had not yet revealed its full extent, so small it still looked, less than a day old, it shadow covering less than a day of my life; and yet its sorrow was to grow and grow as far as the future should extend.

The day cleared in the afternoon and the wind dropped;

and against the empty horizon I saw at last Gavin's boat nearing the shore. It slowly grew and grew, like a death-ship in a dream; and at last the dinghy was lowered that brought him to the strand. He already knew; and, bowed with a single grief, we sat side by side beside the dark brown waters of the empty burn where no animal companion delighted us with his greeting. Neither Gavin nor I had yet realized that the blow so suddenly struck had ended a world; nor that the very grief we at that moment shared was to divide us.

From that time when we sat by the burn together our roles (as I had conceived them) were reversed; it was I who was abased, humiliated, exposed, shamed, Gavin who was the giver; and with a magnanimity the situation evoked from him, he offered me forgiveness, compassion, he accepted a part of the blame; he showed in himself, in this shadowy enactment of the old story of the lost garden, the innate nobility of Adam, as like Eve I wept. But I could not sustain my abasement; my pride in having been, as I had thought, the doer of good towards Gavin, blinded me now to the truth, that it lay in my power to do him a greater good, by accepting a humiliation, in allowing him to take from me the part on which I had so prided myself. I could not abdicate, I could not endure my new role as the blame-worthy and the weak; I could not help Gavin any more because I could not let him help me.

Neither then nor thereafter, neither from Gavin, from myself, nor from the divine world, could I accept forgive-ness. Refusing forgiveness I refused love. I chose punish-ment because I could not bear to be forgiven. I had tried to win love by deserving it, but I could not accept it on the only terms reality permits, as something which can be given but never deserved. I felt safer with punishment; for retribution belongs to the order of cause and effect, the law of karma, which gives us our deserts.

'God is love,' Gavin had once said to me, calling me to task for some hardening of the heart against the pain of wounded pride. And now my pride finally chose the way of remorse because I could not endure the other. So I went away burdened by the guilt of my deed; on my head Gavin's life-blood with the blood of his animal soul; for perhaps I did him an injury from which he could not ever wholly recover. I do not know what expiation I imagined could ever free me from such guilt; but knew that whatever punishment should be laid on me I must bear. It seemed to me mere sentimentality to seek exoneration by imagining I might be 'forgiven' by God or man for evil brings its inevitable consequences, and so long as these continue to operate we cannot be freed. By these consequences we must abide, as effect follows cause; endeavouring, at all events, to weave no more spells, to set in operation no more causes whose effects may extend beyond our power to undo what we have done. I could only accept as just my banishment, and bear the consequences of past actions, my own and those of others (who like myself had set in motion chains of causality which would break their hearts too were they to know their progressions) without complaint.

Perhaps the guilt I incurred towards Gavin is not the greatest of the evils of which I am guilty; but, unlike other chains of causality which I may have set in motion, this one was plain to be seen, and had come about in spite of the greatest effort of which I was capable, to do all right in a relationship which I valued supremely.

Many years later I had a dream that in the garden of the new house I had just taken was 'the ancestral fountain'. It was like the well at Bavington, but choked with dead leaves, and with living weeds. The dead leaves I removed easily, but the weeds were so deeply rooted I could not tear them out. Nevertheless the water that rose continually from its hidden source was pure; and in it I washed a new-born child. How many myths tell of the same reality as that dream I have since realized; Porphyry's cave of the nymphs, where the waters of generation rise in the inaccessible darkness of the world-cave; Spenser's spring of sorrow where a nymph of

81

stone pours water which cannot wash the blood from the hands of the new-born infant of Mordant and Amavia; the Christian font and the mysterious rite of baptism. The symbol of my dream was realized when my grandson was baptized; and in the garden where in my dream I had seen the fountain, all his living ancestors were gathered; my parents, and my children and other grandparents bringing other chains of causality unknown; all those whose failures and misdeeds, whose unrealized aspirations and stifled desires he must inherit; a burden unknown to him that he must carry, and of which a part is mine. And the new-born child was held in the arms of the old, who wished him only some unknown good, beyond whatever portion each must pass on to him of original sin. Which is the stronger, the tangled weaving of destiny, the navel cord, cause and effect and inheritance, or the grace of that water rising always pure from a source deeper than the roots of those weeds?

*

Not the least terrible aspect of that disaster was, to me, that catastrophe had struck at the time when at every moment of every hour of those last days at Sandaig, all my thought was turned towards the source: was that catastrophe an answer to my prayer, or a rejection of it? Was the answer to my invocation of that world the destruction of an earthly paradise? But it was not mine only, but Gavin's that had been destroyed. It is pleasant to do good to others, terrible to see ourselves as the causes of suffering, but is not that too a kind of pride? As to the catastrophe to Gavin, for that too my pride assumed perhaps a responsibility which was inordinate; forgetting that his destiny too must lie in God's hands and not (for all the instrumental part, both for good and ill that I had played in it) in mine. Or was I in fact rejected at that gate because, giving all my love and all my thought to Gavin I was neglecting other duties? Putting that love before my children's good? Beofre my duty to my parents? The truth is never simple; of all these threads, and others unknown to me, my fate was woven. But at the time and for years after I could see only desolation and remorse, and I turned away from the interior world in a mechanical stupor of misery.

Exile, then, began; for Gavin, I believe, as well as for myself. Did the first man and woman know the very instant at which the gates of Paradise were closed against them? Could they at first believe they were closed for ever? For those gates are invisible to the eye; all looked as it had done the day before, every intricate form of leaf and tree, cloud and island, bird and beast. The burn flowed on, its brown water dancing as before, and the silver ring of the sea still shone as brightly as always. The golden flowers bloomed still, and the scent of the young birch-leaves was sweet on the air. Only the gates were closed that shut the spiritual world off from nature, empty now of life and sweetness. And yet, sitting with Gavin by the burn, I was still incredulous; it could not be that a world was so suddenly gone. Nor could I realize that I had myself brought all this about—for how easily could I justify each act, invoke chance or accident, and disclaim responsibility! But knowing as I did that thoughts are agents of power, whose tides and currents ebb and flow invisibly, I knew that what had come about was fate not chance; yet still I could not believe that never again would that loved place be Eden.

> Push'd by the horned flood, and all its trees adrift,
> The haunt of orcs and seales and sea-mew's clang
> To teach man that God attributes to place
> No sanctity, if none be thither brought.

*

I think I forfeited my relationship with Gavin not with my heart's cry, or curse, whichever it may have been; nor even when I lost Mij. It was when I refused—when in pride I could not accept—his forgiveness. I had become habituated to thinking of myself in the role of the giver, the helper. I

83

clung to that role in part from self-righteousness, in part from fear of losing him; only by being needed, I thought, could I hope to be wanted. That, of course, is one of the dangers of a relationship in which physical attraction plays no part; and any woman in a similar situation should guard against it. How blind I was! How it must have irked him to see in me the resolute, the over-strained determination always to be the giver, always to be the strong one! My pride and my self-righteousness, of which I was so culpably oblivious, how clear to him! And perhaps equally if I had helped him really, must he have felt at a disadvantage. For we love those to whom we give, not those who are forever giving to us; for one very obvious reason, that in giving we see ourselves in so flattering a light. And is that not one reason why selfish people are so attractive? Less cynically said, they bring out the best in ourselves. But now it was for me to say 'Gavin forgive me' and to accept in our relationship the part of the guilty one, the needy one, open to his compassion and his pardon; that he had been, by the burn that day, so generously ready to give. But I could not play that part; I was prostrated with remorse, bewildered and paralysed. In my remorse I could see no way of helping Gavin or doing him any good again. And yet in letting him forgive me and responding to that forgiveness I might have given him a gift of more value than all my supposed 'help'.

Anna was now at Cambridge, James doing his National Service; and I had arranged with Gavin that he should rent the two lower floors of 9 Paultons Square; there Mij would have had access to the garden; Gavin had already built a tank for him. But that plan, made in happiness, was fulfilled in sorrow. When Gavin moved into my house Mij was already dead.

For the next year Gavin and I, stunned though we both were, tried to remain as if friends; learning only little by little the extent of our devastation. I had no longer the power to comfort him and lived only in remorse; not daring even to pray, since disaster had come at a time when I had turned my thoughts so sincerely—I must even now say I was sincere—to a renewal of my determination to live my life according to the divine will. But now, to see Gavin was to weep; not a few tears, but streaming rivers of tears that would not stop, that I could no more control than the waters of a swollen burn. And that no man can bear. I who formerly had, or seemed to have, so magical a power to succour Gavin, now had no power at all.

One thing I did not tell—could not bring myself to tell— when I wrote this record of old sorrows. But now a memory rises from its grave and returns to me. I was still, then, living in the top flat of 9 Paultons Square, and Gavin and I had not quite lost hope that something might remain. I had been sitting with him in the room that was now his; sadly conversing, it must have been, like Adam and Eve after the Fall. It comes to my mind that he asked me, then, to share his bed with him, as once before; to cast off our defensive armour, to lay down our weapons. And I did not do so. Sadly, slowly, I climbed the stairs to my own lonely bed, leaving him to his own. Knowing that I could no longer, now, give him either help or comfort.

*

I was at that time living, during term, at Girton; and when on Muriel Bradbrook's invitation, I took up my modest Research Fellowship at my old College, it had seemed no longer necessary to keep the whole of 9 Paultons Square. Now it seemed the same inevitability that had formerly brought us together was to divide us; and all our plans and good intentions were whirled away like bubbles on that dark stream which was sweeping us apart.

I do not know—I shall never know—what Gavin's truth was, nor how long before I realized it he had shut the invisible gates of his life against me, presenting to me, instead, a merely external and social mask. Perhaps there was no absolute moment at which this was so. But I could no longer continue to deceive myself after a certain evening we spent together once when I had come up from Cambridge. How the storm came to break I do not remember, nor does the occasion matter. But I do remember how, sitting in the Berkeley buttery, Gavin laid at my charge fault after fault (including my dress and my physical appearance), blameworthy action upon blameworthy action; most with enough semblance of justification to leave me stripped of every defence; and yet blind love had seen another truth, or those truths otherwise. Against such a presentation of truth as falsehood, or falsehood as truth, or simply of another truth than mine, I was defenceless, and unstanchable tears poured from my eyes (another fault unpardonable by Gavin's code) making me loathsome to behold. The truth of the heart only God can judge; I remember saying this to Gavin at last—that he and I would have to stand the judgement of the God within. Certainly I did not defend myself; for 'the truth' is not an abstract proposition which can be reached by argument but only the aspect persons and events have in living minds.

He left me, at last, at the door of the friend's house with whom I was spending the night. He so far realized my extremity on that occasion as to telephone Canetti and say, 'If Kathleen has killed herself, I shall never forgive her.' But Kathleen has neither the courage nor, ultimately, the despair of the suicide. Fortitude is to me second nature; even, an excess, a kind of outer insensibility, a false strength assumed when weakness might have been better.

But I saw Gavin the next day; and he assured me he had not meant one half of what he had said; and I replied that of course I had never supposed that he had. But, again, his words had come up from the depths, the fiery pits and deserts which lie as far beyond our everyday selves as does Paradise. Both of us were glad enough to rest in the everyday, like dreamers who return to prosaic morning from places of experience too terrible to contemplate. But these things had been said; and I began to wonder—the thought came to me first as a hypothesis which I did not expect to see proved—rather the reverse—whether I ought to withdraw from Gavin's life; to discover, at least, if he wished me to do so. I therefore pretended to Gavin that I was thinking of giving up 9 Paultons Square altogether. This was plausible enough; for now that I had rooms in College I could say that (my son being on the point of marrying), I no longer needed a house at all. I thought he would say 'No, no, please don't leave London altogether, I need you.' But he did not say it. Then I began, as it were, to pay out more rope; asked if he would like to take over the lease of my house; I doubted, I said, whether I could afford to renew it. (I had at that time the new lease in my hands, made out in my name and ready to sign.) He said he would like it. I expected him to say, 'But where will you live? You cannot bury yourself in a women's College.' ('It was like seeing Achilles in Hades, finding you here' was Stanley Spencer's remark to me when he came to paint his portrait of the Mistress of Girton.) But Gavin did not say it. I paid out all the rope I had; and such was my grief that he took it all that I had no heart to wish to keep anything for myself; I could not defend myself against him, for I had made his interest my own even against myself. My sense of guilt towards Gavin for the loss of our beloved Mij was so great that I felt a certain respite from remorse in whatever restitution it was in my power to make; and all I had was my precarious tenancy of the house which had come to me with a friend's blessing. Even so, at the last moment, when it had been agreed that Gavin, not I, should take over the house, and a new lease was to be made out in his name, I suddenly thought that it was too much, that it was as unfitting that I should give, as that Gavin should take, all I had in the world. I wrote to him asking if, instead of his being my tenant, I could be his: could I keep the little flat at the top of the house? But to that letter I received no answer.

If I had read Aristotle's *Ethics* at that time, I would have understood that, in bringing about a situation in which

Gavin behaved badly towards me I was in fact not preserving, as I had despairingly hoped, whatever remained of a friendship in decline, but making it impossible for any friendship to exist at all; for countless instances have proved the philosopher right when he says we can forgive those who have injured us, but never those whom we have injured; since the former enable us to see ourselves in a favourable light, the latter force us to see ourselves unfavourably.

All this Canetti knew, step by step; my motives, my hopes and fears, I told him all as it befell and showed him the letters I received from Gavin. He was much concerned about what I was doing: probably he tried to dissuade me; but I could not defend myself against Gavin when I was myself fighting on his side. Even from Canetti I probably disguised (speaking plausibly enough of economy) the fact that to give up 9 Paultons Square was the thing I least wanted to do in the world. I could not even now relinquish the belief that at some point Gavin would say, 'You have gone far enough away now, don't go out of my life altogether.' But at no point did he call me back, or so much as ask me what I would do; this, it seemed, did not any longer concern him. Still, he invited me to visit him, when the house was no longer mine but his, and asked me to admire his alterations and furniture. It was too much, and those unstanchable tears flowed again so that I had to go away. I sat alone in a corner of the Blue Cockatoo restaurant, where there were candles on the tables, and dark shadows, and tried to regain command of myself before returning by a late train to Cambridge. Gavin had rid himself of me; with my own cooperation and help, be it said—the last good it lay in my power to do him.

One might suppose that by now I had understood that Gavin wished me out of his life altogether. But love is slow to understand such simple, self-evident things. Because the truth of the vision I had seen possessed a reality incommeasurable with this shadow-world in which Gavin and I

88

now seemed to struggle as in a dream, I believed that, if I could only somehow get back to that truth, it must prevail; for I had never forgotten that anamnesis, nor could I believe that Gavin, either, could forget what once we had seemed to share.

Once more, and for the last time, I visited Gavin in the room where Cooie Lane had first taken me into the protection of her house; the room that had been mine, where I had lived and written and that had been my children's home. There the superimposed images of memory were all adrift; for it was to this room, too, that Tambi had first brought Gavin to visit me, and where Gavin had said, 'It is as if a goddess had turned her head and looked at me.' There my life, such as it was, had been lived. How it was, on this occasion, that I broke my bitter silence and spoke of the unanswered letter in which I had asked Gavin if I could keep, as his tenant, the two small top rooms, I do not know; but when I did so, he exclaimed, 'The unposted letter!' For his reply, written months before, had just been found by Mary, at Sandaig, unposted, in the jacket pocket of the boy to whom it had been entrusted. Gavin had, of course, said that I could keep the flat. 'But what else could I have said?' he exclaimed. 'After all, I am a gentleman.' Not a very warm reply, I realized, upon reflection; but at the time I laughed and said, 'I thought you *capable de tout*!' and hope rose again.

And those missing letters—Tess of the d'Urbeville's, pushed under the carpet, and all those others whose miscarriage seems to have changed lives, are not they too mislaid by the daimons? I had been glad enough to cry miracle when the two hands were joined together; but when by those same hands we were torn apart, I was reluctant to see the same mind, the same purpose at work. I wrote to Gavin from Cambridge, saying how infinitely rather I would lose my house than lose his friendship. I desperately believed that, since that lost letter had been written, every wound was healed, every rift mended. Perhaps even I thought I had by now bought, at the price of my house, at the price of the discretion of my withdrawal, a renewed lease of friendship.

I see now that it was because of Gavin's desire that I should not remain at 9 Paultons Square that I left, and not because of a missing letter. Who knows how such losses came about; just as, step by step, I acted in such a way as to bring about the death of Mij, whom Gavin and I equally loved, perhaps Gavin also brought it about that the letter was lost. Message-bearers are quick to act upon almost imperceptible signs, expressions, moods which communicate that a letter is tiresome, written reluctantly; or urgent, vital. Had Gavin been anxious I should receive it he would have impressed upon his messenger that it was an important letter and must go off at once. There had been a time when he would have telephoned; the cost of trunk-calls from Scotland to Cambridge would never, for Gavin, have been a reason for writing a letter instead.

Perhaps Gavin was embarrassed by the coming to light of the letter and by my boundless joy and relief at the possibility of still continuing to imagine that all had not been lost; for he asked me, once again, to revisit Sandaig. Or perhaps he too hoped that all might not be lost; for I never yet knew Gavin to do anything except because he wanted to do it. In that lay a great part of his charm, for it gave to all his actions an authenticity, an absence of pretence or hypocrisy. When, long before, he had sent me to his house I had known, being there, that he had wanted me to be there; when he no longer wanted me he could make that, too, perfectly clear. And so, hoping perhaps against hope that from the wreckage and desolation something might yet be saved, I went for the last time down the familiar path which for me led to that centre which unreason still called home when reason knew it was not so. So a bird will fly to the place where a felled tree stood. There is for each creature an invisible thread, or beam, which draws it home; and for me the thread drew me still to Gavin's rowan-tree between the waterfall of the burn with its fringe of birch

90

and alder, and the strand where plover and sanderling ran on their rapid feet. But now I found that Gavin had built about his house that palisade of high wooden palings of which I had dreamed years before; it had been built to keep in the other otters he now had at Sandaig. I went through the visible gate, indeed; but by invisible gates I was barred out; a gate was closed within every bud on every twig of birch and alder, closed in rock and water and fern and heather-sweet air, closed in sky and sea and the line of the hills of Skye, in the grey rocks by the shore where I went alone to weep comfortless tears near the last place where I had seen our dear animal angel swim away.

It is said in Celtic countries that a death appears first in the sky, then little by little its darkness descends until at last it touches the earth, and becomes a reality in this world. In the invisible air it gathers, to rain down its shower of blood. When I left Mary's cottage where I was to sleep, to go down the track to Gavin's house, I seemed to be repelled as by the intangible negative force of a magnetic field. I seemed to wade through lead, as in a dream; to be enveloped in a heavy darkness, as if the death I had caused still hung there, or some greater evil to come. Through that repelling cloud I forced my way; and again, for the last time, Gavin tried, I think, to comfort me; not any more as someone in his life, but just because my grief remained as a last bond, which he would gladly break. Yet there was, even so, for one last moment a return of old love; walking back with me as far as the bridge over the burn, he said, 'We will never doubt one another again, never, never;' and I replied, 'Never, never.' Yet the very next day, the tension grown too great for either of us to bear, we parted in anger, each knowing there could be no return, that we had both been hurt too deeply. As I left the house I had said I would not communicate with him again. 'Oh yes you will,' he had said; 'you will write me yet another letter of reconciliation.' For that is what I had done, from Girton, after the discovery of the missing letter had seemed in a gleam of false hope to promise that all might yet be well. It seems that my letter had served only to put Gavin into the embarrassing position of having to respond; now his words made it impossible for me ever to write to him again.

My last memory of Sandaig is one of an overwhelming woe, not for myself but because I seemed to see Gavin, without me, abandoned to a losing battle against circumstances already so weighted against him—otter-boys unreliable if only because they were young; loneliness in that region of imagination we had shared. I knew that I could have—should have—been able to help him to turn these desperate odds; that I still could have done so. If only I could have somehow brushed away some invisible cobweb of illusion and misunderstanding, we should still have been companions, bearing one another's burdens. For we both had heavy burdens to carry, lonely lives to lead. Yet though I felt so desperate and so clear-sighted a pity, I could not speak. Did I lack the courage? Or did I know, then, with the same clairvoyance, that it would be useless? I do not know. Perhaps it was pride, perhaps despair that kept me silent, then and on other occasions when I longed to speak the words that were in my heart. 'Gavin, I love you, let me stay in your life, let me share your burdens, even now, as I long to do.' Why does love keep silent when it should speak? But I have been able to speak from my heart only in my poems.

Gavin had, on that last visit of mine to Sandaig, another otter, Edal; not so dear as Mijbil, but at all events an otter. Now she was ill, so gravely ill that he thought her dying. My last act before I left was an attempt towards expiation. One practical thing I did, which I hoped and believed might help her recover; and in the night after our last parting, as I lay in Mary's cottage in grief, I made one last bargain with the dark angel at the barred gate. 'Let her recover,' I said 'and I will never seek to see Gavin again.' It is certain she recovered; far from certain that my prayer had anything to do with it. Yet at the time it was as if dark wings had taken it and carried it from me, like the beating, living heart of those sacrificed to the gods. To give one's heart to be torn out can comfort when comfort cannot. To the lost, mercy, human or divine, is of all things the most unendurable. I asked for none, and had none on myself.

I kept my vow; hoping still that Gavin might again seek me out, or the one mind bring us together again. That mind can play strange tricks; for when I went to order a name-plate for my new house (for I had taken a house again, in Paultons Square, in the brief period of hope, after learning about the missing letter, that Gavin and I might be friends again, as formerly), the ironmonger from a box of samples drew a brass plate on which his name was engraved: Gavin Maxwell; as if the living bond between us could still un-erringly seek out such fragments of a broken world. I heard from him at last; he wrote to tell me he was getting married. When I read that letter I had no longer anything to hope or fear in this world. From that time I felt only one compelling need—to see my life as a whole, to read the pages of my own Book of Judgement; to understand, perhaps, what is written there. Then, perhaps, I might be free.

I can call one witness in my defence: Helen Sutherland, when I read to her the passage about the curse evoked by the Tree—if curse it was, for I did not see it as such, it was a desperate heart's cry for truth—understood. 'You wanted him to *see*,' she said. I had written the story in her house, in the little white bedroom that was for me in all these years a sanctuary in the house of a friend who did value me, who would not have recognized in me the image that I had begun to feel, obscurely, that Gavin had of me. Which is not of course to say that he was entirely wrong. Yet Helen, with her great intelligence, her sense of Christian justice and mercy, and her respect for the best in all of us who were her friends, did see.

When I called for the loosing of the lightning from the tree, I was in a state of unreasoning anguish; yet as I look back now on the flaming anger of that evening when I cried out for the Eumenides, it was, I know, a last and desperate cry for the triumph of the holy and the beautiful world over the vulgar and the superficial. As I stand before those immortal living presences, both the dark and the bright, I would plead that the root of my anger was a desire for the holy reality to prevail. The psalmist was not afraid to invoke the divine justice in its terrible aspect; 'Let God arise and let his enemies be scattered' is a prayer that arises from the depths of a terrible purity. I did not, God knows, wish to injure Gavin or to destroy him—only that he should not be allowed to forget the vision I thought he had all but lost. But it is not the way of that world to bend the will, which is at all times free to turn away; only at the Last Judgement must every soul face the God within. In that world there may be no difference in value between the divine mercy and the divine anger; but who is pure enough to dare to invoke that world's vengeance? It may be that oblivion of the soul calls, before the tribune of the gods, for the awakening lightning; the only aspect the divine mercy can assume in the face of our extreme resistance; for that oblivion is a spiritual state more deadly than any suffering which may serve to awaken us from it. Yet those who cry, as I did, for justice, cannot afterwards beg for mercy; I invoked the most terrible epiphany of all; and perhaps my prayer was answered.

*

The Lion's Mouth

THAT GOLDEN string which had once (or so I imagined) united me with Gavin had become a severed
cord from whose living substance my life bled away
continually, so that I lost all power to lift up my heart; and
this for several years during which I did not see him. Of these
years one memory will serve for all: the hired car standing
outside what had been my own house to take the groom to
his wedding. For what seemed unrelated reasons, I had
passed the end of Paultons Square at that time of all times.
'The marriage-hearse' was the phrase that came to my mind.
Of course, I may only have imagined that the car had come
for Gavin; but that he married on that day, that I did not
imagine.

He had sent me an invitation to the large reception to be
held a few days later; and I even wondered whether, so that
his friends and mine should know that he was marrying
with my good will, and himself feel no shadow of trouble
on my account I ought to compel myself to go. It was John
Hayward who brought me to my senses, pointing out that
a man on the eve of his wedding would be thinking of his
bride, not of me at all; that his guests and hers would be
from a world in which my very existence would be unknown; that my presence would be neither here nor there.
'No one, after all, ever imagined Gavin would marry *you*,'
John concluded. Illogically it was John whom I did not
forgive; I took his salutary advice but did not see him again
for two years.

(Only in this cold January of 1976 can I bring myself to
face a memory I had not recorded. Before I had left Paultons

Square I had been warned; but had put away the warning. Gavin had said to me, one day, that he had been thinking of marrying; I did not take this very seriously at the time, and indeed nothing came of it then. But he had spoken very gently to me, saying, 'I would like you to accept my wife, as you are the two people who know me best.' I had not responded to that request directly, but had said, also so quietly, more to myself than to him, that he may no more have noted my words than I his—on both sides it seemed as though we were each speaking to ourselves, not to one another, 'Then I will go away.' I could not believe it; and yet that is what I did; I withdrew myself from Gavin's life, little by little, always hoping to be recalled; and I was not recalled.

Yet I had waited. Someday, someday I would surely hear from him, or meet him. And one day his letter came, and my heart gave a leap of joy to see the familiar hand-writing Then I read it; he was going to marry a friend of many years; she had been married to a friend of Gavin's but was now free; a woman of his own world, of course. The letter asked me, again, to accept and love for his sake, his wife.

Gavin's letter reached me when I was staying with Willa Muir in the house at Swaffham Prior where she and Edwin had lived for a few happy years until Edwin's death in 1961. I had given up my Research Fellowship at Girton, grateful as I had been for Muriel Bradbrook's kindness in inviting me back to my old College, there to continue in some financial security my work on Blake.

I am sure my natural friends must have thought it a pity that I could not have settled in Academe, that happy, civilized world, where work so valuable may be done, in a freedom unimaginable elsewhere. I enjoyed teaching the young, too, although this never presented itself to me as my task in life. Why could I not have done so? I enjoyed many friendships, too, in Cambridge. C. S. Lewis arrived in Cambridge in the same year as myself, to take up his Regius Professorship; installed in those same rooms in Magdalene where so many years before William Empson had been my host; now it was C. S. Lewis—not sitting on the windowbox, but standing with, on one side Owen Barfield and on the other A. C. Harwood, the Anthroposophist; like three Eldils from one of his own science fictions. Tom Henn, too, who read Yeats to us in what an Irishman in Sligo called 'his great cathedral voice that comes from the heart;' there was Muriel Bradbrook herself; and many peripheral figures who adorned that world. It was partly through myself, and also through John Holloway and David Daiches, that Edwin and Willa themselves came to settle at Swaffham Prior; Edwin was honoured by the University with a Doctor's degree; and he came often to visit Muriel Bradbrook and myself at Girton. It all seemed so perfect.

When my friend Rafael Nadal (Lorca's closest friend, and a member of that group of Spanish Intellectuals whose master had been Unamuno; Bunuel and Salvador Dali had been of his circle) came to visit me, 'What a *beautiful* room,' he had exclaimed with that Spanish enthusiasm of his; then added, 'you *must* get away from here!' A spiritual friend. He was right, of course. If the record of my life shows any pattern is it not a series of returns to the wild places? I am wild and of the wilds, the inspirers meet me there; only there am I not, in some measure, an exile, playing (however enjoyably) a part.

My scholarship was always incidental to the needs of the poet for knowledge of a certain kind. Like Thomas Taylor, I read the books of wisdom for the sake of that wisdom, seeing scholarship always as a means to an end, never as an end in itself. But it is I suppose before all else the needs of the poet that have driven me away from those 'straight roads' made by education. My war-job at Bush House seemed more like a fantastic dream than a reality; the British Council still more so. My attempts to Christianise myself have all failed; and now Academe. I felt, in some indescribable way, in a false position; just as I had felt with the Church. My friends were poets and painters, all wild like

97

myself; not, Bohemia—I seldom set foot in any 'pub', and then only as the guest of Louis MacNeice or some other— and I do not enjoy that dropping of barriers of the world where 'poets' (usually very minor ones, for any serious artist must live a life in some sense disciplined) move in a kind of promiscuous gregariousness. My personal life was never at any time, after I had left Charles, emotionally involved within 'the literary world', with which my relations were so to say professional. But every true poet is wild in a different way. David Jones, in his magical room in Harrow; 'He still lives in a dug-out,' I remember someone saying of him with much perception. Winifred Nicholson belonged to Cumberland and its luminous grey skies. Edwin and Willa floated like clouds among us. 'Edwin will never go into anything unless he can see *an out*,' Willa once said. Dylan Thomas, it is true, was the typical poet of the pubs, although even he did not write his poems in that Dionysiac world, but in his native Wales. His friend Vernon Watkins was quietly wild on his headland on the Gower Peninsula; he too had fled from Cambridge many years before.

Eliot, indeed, from his office in Russell Square wore the impeccable mask of the distinguished publisher and man of letters he was; but was there not some truth in Tambi's words, 'But he is really a wild man, like me.'? The poet must protect his wildness as best he may, with whatever camouflage he can create; a principle inherited from the shy animal world from a millennial past. And for a poet whose theme was the city, the city, also, must be his protective disguise.

Not living poets only, or principally, but the dead also are, in that sense, our own people in a way that for the critic is not so. The critic's work begins where the work of the poet ends—with 'the words on the page'; and the processes of commentary are far other than those of formulating some mood or vision or realization, one of those instantaneous intellections that come with a leap of the heart or a flash of imagination. When the words are on the page the poet's work is done; in the hope that the words may evoke in the reader the same flash, or mood, or intellection; and on the whole the simpler the reader the more likely this is to take place; and the best of critics—Coleridge is of course the best of critics—can help the reader towards this. Some years ago, to make more room on my bookshelves I threw out (not literally, of course: I sold them) all works of criticism not written by poets. Scholarship is another matter, and works of scholarship I did not throw out. I remember 'Jack' Lewis asking me once if I had ever found myself helped in my appreciation of any work of literature by any work of criticism; and when I said no, never, he said that neither had he. So perhaps I was not wrong in being unable to breathe the cold dry air of a Cambridge still in so many ways dominated by the kind of thought—and indeed by the same people—as I had encountered in my student days.

Cambridge soil may be fertile enough, but my own native Grass of Parnassus will not grow in those English gardens. Or was there in me some lack of adaptability, of some quite simple human trait that would have enabled me there to take root; as I think Muriel Bradbrook would have liked me to do? At all events, she gave me the chance.

So in Girton I could not, the second time more than the first, take root. Some homing instinct had taken me back to Paultons Square as the only place left where I might still pick up the threads of the broken pattern of my life, and I had already taken the lease of the house (no longer No. 9) that is still mine; though it has never seemed, in quite the same way, home. But I had let the house for the months I was to spend in America to give my Andrew Mellon lectures on Blake at the National Gallery in Washington; and now, at the beginning of a new Academic year, I was staying as Willa's guest until the time for departure. How happy Priory Cottage had been, while Edwin lived; how often had I, alone or with Muriel, taken the 'bus that dropped us by those two churches at Swaffham Prior, where the pigeons and the jackdaws, much to Edwin and Willa's delight and

99

amusement, disputed the two towers. Now Willa was alone. I had seen her, at Edwin's funeral, stricken with grief, and looking ready to throw herself into the grave with her beloved Edwin. But she had begun to live again, to build up a world with her cat Popsy, and the various visiting cats, like 'Johnnie the Vicar' with his 'face like a chrysanthemum', as Willa said. She fed all who came through the cat-door in the kitchen. Willa had the gift of creating round herself a 'little' world alongside the main world, of cats, jackdaws, cleaning-women and tradesmen's boys, a fine firm bright texture of all the little daily things. But the centre of it all was Popsy and the rhythm of her saucers, exits, entrances, privileges, and daily rounds of house and garden. Living, then, with Willa, I understood very well how she had sustained Edwin. She and he had cared little for necessities, but much for small luxuries. Willa made 'drop-scones' fresh and hot; drank only the best tea (blended by herself in varying proportions from a family of tea-caddies) properly made with boiling water in a heated teapot; kept a bottle of Drambuie, from which she gave us tiny drams in the Bohemian glasses she and Edwin had brought with them from Czechoslovakia; could eat only the freshest and cleanest of food, though the dust lay thick under the bookcases. She was, as I often told her, like the Princess who could not sleep because of a pea hidden under nine mattresses; if I made the tea, she could tell to a tealeaf if my blending had been ill done. She had, besides, a gift which should be, but seldom is, accounted one of woman's greatest beauties— the softness of her touch. She could always, so she said, 'gentle' Edwin with the caress of her hand, with its fine tapering fingers. My mother's hands, too, had that soft, thrilling gentleness. One of my three granddaughters inherits it, though I do not.

'I'm soft-centred,' she used to say; some, who had hoped to talk with Edwin, were daunted by her aggressive conversational manner; but was she not, perhaps, just the protector of his silences that Edwin needed? A dragon to strangers, but to him, gentleness itself? 'Edwin had all the best of me,' she used to say; for him she had been—and knew she had been—a person she could never be for any other, because only Edwin, whom she loved, could evoke that side of her. And in their wandering homeless life, she said, 'my home was Edwin's bosom'.

I was with Willa, then, on the morning when that letter came; and when I had read it, her gentle hand comforted me. Later I was with Helen, and she, too, was infinitely compassionate and gentle. But it was Willa (who in any case on principle always took the woman's side) who comforted me then. I remember mechanically taking the 'bus into Cambridge, as I had planned to do, to work, I suppose, at the University library. I remember walking round the market, looking for I knew not what, and buying for myself a little necklace of mother-of-pearl beads; Sandaig shore, Sandaig shells. I remember that I could not swallow—could scarcely swallow for several days. However our grief may be self-caused, self-inflicted, and deserved, how we suffer! What a capacity for suffering a human being has! And I suffered to the extreme limit of my capacity. Yet fortitude had long been with me so habitual that I carried on with my life. I could not break down if I tried, so habitual with me has it become, in the course of a life in which I have carried my own burdens, to go on, from day to day. Perhaps, like my father, I am very strong physically; but also it is hard to break down when there is no one there to pick us up again. I remember Willa saying (and we had been speaking of Gavin), 'What a wonderful thing it is that men and women mean so much to one another!' And indeed it is so; immeasurably much, whether in a relationship, like her own with Edwin, cemented by mutual love; or no less in a doomed relationship like my own with Gavin. For even though I can now see how at every step I acted blindly and selfishly, God knows he was everything to me.

For the last day or two before embarking on the Queen Mary on my passage to New York I was staying with Rupert

101

and Helen Gleadow, in their flat in Cheyne Row, just round the corner from Paulton's Square; and on the day after Gavin's marriage I sailed. Among the first-class passsengers (thank God I was in the Cabin class) was that very friend Gavin had brought to Sandaig on the fatal day of the rowan-tree.

I went to face the world as a scholar, a moment of success come at last, in a state of all but unbearable suffering. How I got through those months, which demanded of me a best I could not, under these circumstances, give, God only knows. By an irony of fate Washington's élite set themselves to welcome and entertain me. My lectures, fortunately, had already been written the previous summer before Gavin's letter-card, telling me of his engagement, had destroyed in me, with the long-nursed hope of ultimate reconciliation, the power to work.

In the night following the day that letter had reached me, as the mortally ill or wounded sometimes experience a partial separation from the suffering bodies they see lying on some bed below as if they themselves were other, I had been able, passing through and beyond my delirium of anguish, to see Gavin and his chosen bride in the full light of a love which had now been put to the test of a total renunciation; (by that paradox by which the beloved asks most of the lover when he asks nothing at all). It had seemed, from that clear solitude above the snow-line of suffering, that I could love for his sake the woman he loved (that was what his brief conventional note had asked of me), that I could be glad he would have children. Perhaps I then allowed myself to fancy, he would bring his wife to visit me, would say to her, 'This is Kathleen, of whom I have told you;' perhaps they would invite me to cross again the threshold of the house that had been mine, to see that first-born for whose sake I would be glad to have lost what I valued most. I had, to Gavin, committed myself absolutely; but this was the one sacrifice I had never expected to be asked to make. Death would have been less painful, and infinitely less humiliating; yet, knowing how Gavin had loved our animal-child, how could I not wish for him a human son? It was as if, during that night, I saw all our lives as from some place beyond these brief life-times as stars sent out from the same source, each in its inmost nature immortal, beautiful, only and for ever to be loved: how then could I hate another woman whose nature was in essence the same as my own, who, loving Gavin, would be giving him the same love of which all are only channels, instruments? As in the order of angels message and messenger are one, so, in that altitude of freedom, I perceived that the ten thousand thousand agents of the one mind come and go within the universal sympathy in which no life or love is separate from the one life in all. In that insight, that freedom from myself, I beheld in that term and source of all existences a profound joy, wherein for a while I seemed almost to participate, as I lay, literally beside myself, outside myself in this almost unendurable confrontation with a reality by which my individual existence seemed in process of destruction.

I wrote, of course, to Gavin; very briefly. In the outer world (as John Hayward in the clear light of that world had pointed out to me) it made little difference what I wrote, or whether I wrote at all. But I had known too long of that second world, invisible to sense, in which thoughts have the reality of things, and acts. It was not enough to write; I must send out to Gavin no deadly thoughts, must lay no curse upon him, or his bride.

One night, in a dream, Gavin's bride came, and kissed me. But upon that exaltation, barely attained and scarcely held, followed mere grief. I lived, through that winter, only in the night, dragging myself through each day to the threshold, there to take up the invisible work which awaited me in an interior country which had no longer any frontier with the outer and common world. I longed for each empty day to end, so that I could resume my task, follow as best I could the bleeding severed thread of my life which led me now, like Blake's 'soul exploring the recesses of the grave' to discover 'the secrets of a land unknown'. I wanted only to be alone, taking up my grief each night, like the woman in the fairy-tale who must spin and weave the nettles that grow on graves into redemptive garments. I strove to learn my sorrow, to understand, to possess myself of it not as pain but as knowledge. Suffering, I was still inhabiting my love; but more than an inability to relinquish drove me on: that was the way the clue led. Into the heart of grief itself I sought to penetrate, as if there I should discover some secret that would resolve all. It was not courage, either (the hope to be free by facing the thing feared); this was my quest, the task love itself had laid upon me, and therefore sacred.

'Il faut que vous mettez la tête dans la gueule du lion,' Alexis Léger said to me, I remember: the advice of the great St. John Perse, author of *Exile*; for whom all the ways of the world lead into the future, open to the conquest of imagination. In the garden of Dumbarton Oaks, on a bench among the violets, it was. I had met him several years before on my first visit to the United States; then as an obscure 'visiting poet', now in a more honourable guise. But he had been kind—more than kind to me on that first visit. I had been the guest of William Empson's brother Charles and his wife Monica, my old neighbour in Martindale years; and I had been taken to call on the poet by Robert Richman, who organized such meetings for poets reading their works at his Institute of Contemporary Arts; which he had founded in admiration of, and with the help of, our dear mutual friend Herbert Read. M. Léger then invited me to lunch, and I was spellbound by his conversation—monologue rather—as vivid and as enthralling as that of Othello and no less full of 'Anthropophagi, and men whose heads do grow beneath their shoulders'—or the like 'marvels' of the world. Some as simple as the fungi whose soil is the glue of posters in the heart of cities; others as rare as some citrous fruit that grows only on one tree, in the Imperial garden of the Chinese Emperor (M. Léger had known China before the

Revolution), of which one cutting was given to I have forgotten whom, and grew now on Bird Island off New Orleans. He was a man more akin to Gavin than any other poet I have known, caring more for the solitary places and the sea, for the marvels of nature, the earth and its teeming inexhaustible fecundity, than for the 'literary world' which he studiously avoided; or the Academic world, in which he refused absolutely to set foot. 'Do you not', I had said to the poet of *Anabase*, 'miss the wildernesses of the earth here in Washington?' And he had pointed to the vultures circling above the city; the wild places are everywhere, he had said, and there are, besides, tracts of earth in the United States as virgin as any on the surface of the moon. It was W. H. Hudson who had told him about the fungi who have made their habitat the glue of posters; Hudson, whom he had met through Conrad, who had in his youth been his friend and admired master. He had wondered that the great writer should have given him his friendship, an obscure young Frenchman of whom no one had heard. Conrad had said—I hope I reproduce the sense, though not the words (he always spoke French though he understood English better than he liked to have it known)—that chance had brought him, and the obligation towards whatever chance brings is absolute. 'You had in common your love of the sea,' I said; for he had been telling me of the harbours of the world known to him as well as to Odysseus—he even knew the Hebrides, Gavin's waters—but he said No, Conrad hated the sea; the sea, for him, was the antagonist, the enemy.

One must never go back, he said; he had himself sailed round the island of Guadeloupe, his native isle, paradise of his boyhood; but he had known that he must not go on shore. One must go on, never looking back; and his wonderful eyes seemed always to see into distances opening before him. Not eyes wonderful to be looked into, but eyes that wonderfully looked out, and far away, beholding 'les merveilles' that the earth everywhere generates.

I had of course no intention of inviting the advances of the poet I consider as the greatest, after the death of Eliot and of Yeats. I belonged to Gavin; Gavin, who on that first visit to the States had driven me to the airport, and who had given me, when we parted, a little cowrie shell from the Sandaig shore. Why do I find it so hard to confess, even now, twenty years later, that I gave that cowrie shell to Alexis Léger? It seemed, then, the only thing I had worthy of him. Yet Gavin's parting gift should not have been given away; again, as I come to write this story, I find that I was the betrayer, not he. The smallest of shells; but symbol of so much.

On my next visit to Washington, M. Léger, called on me at once; and we always met, thereafter, and were fellow guests both at the house of Francis and Margaret Biddle (the poetess Margaret Chapin) and of Mildred Woods Bliss. Now, among the violets in those beautiful gardens of Dumbarton Oaks I poured out to him my grief. He had admonished me, on a previous occasion, to live like a poet; for to be a poet, he reminded me, is a way of life; not to him would I have had to explain why I could not live in Cambridge. We are not poets, he reminded me, merely when we are writing verse; our imagination must at all times be attuned to the imagination of the world as it flows on, ceaselessly, into the future. It comforted me a little that, scorned by Gavin ('nobody ever thought he would marry *you*') I found that St. John Perse was so real a friend; and he told me to put my head in the lion's mouth.

A few days later, carrying out from one of Washington's dazzling assemblies our champagne onto the terrace, I seemed, with the lights of the city outspread below like a tray of jewels, in the unknown night of the world's spaces, in the company of the poet for whom the earth is itself like a region of the imagination, to stand poised on the brink of Plato's 'moving image of eternity'; we ourselves, and the assembly behind us, uplifted on the bright crest of the world's ever-advancing wave. To those who can relinquish the past—and how much had Alexis Léger relinquished—was not this vision of the future the reward? The former Minister of France's foreign affairs had relinquished more than a private past, a private sorrow; though doubtless these also. Yet I could not let go. Like Lot's wife, I was bound to the past.

Nor did I, after all, go into the arena to meet the lion face to face; and through cowardice, was only mauled by it. Gay Taylor assured me that, astrologically, she thought it more than unlikely that Gavin's marriage would last; and I am bound to admit that I waited for it to end. She had proved right, God knows, in foreseeing sorrow as the outcome of our meeting. But could I not, perhaps, outwait the stars? I was, besides, the prey of an invincible incredulity. When I heard from Canetti that Gavin's brief marriage was in fact over, I said, as I remember, 'God is not merciful but He is just.' Canetti, who could not bring himself to admit any good in the Demiurge nevertheless replied, with a certain solemnity, 'I would not say that; but there is a law.' Only then was I able to take up my life again. I could have listened to many stories current at the time of the explosive break-up of that marriage, but I refused to do so. I remember one, however—from Canetti. Gavin's wife had said to him 'But you are treating me just as you treated Kathleen!' No doubt she had thought, as I had thought, that she, unlike all others who had failed, could meet his needs. I found comfort, even companionship, in that reported phrase.

And what if Gavin's marriage had been under a blessing, if that child for whose sake I could not have withheld the consent of my love, had become a reality? Would I then have been glad, at last? God knows; 'there is a Law', and the outcome was what it was. For the marriage to have been under a blessing, for that son to have been born, everything would have had to be different, not just some one or other element in the situation. And in that case I might have been, at last, glad with him, and for him. I do not know; for I was not put to that test. But I think I would have loved

Gavin's child, had I been given the smallest opportunity to do so.

Neither was my incredulity, perhaps, mere egoism; in it there may have been insight too, the knowledge that no one can with impunity snatch from life anything and everything; we must know what is ours.

What I could not face, then and for long after, was the realization that the One Mind that brought us together, had also parted us. I swung, instead, between the extremes of my despair: the useless protest that since Gavin and I had been to one another Heaven-sent, it could only be by a miscarriage of divine justice that we were parted; and the retrospective denial of what had been. I reached a point when I seemed dispossessed even of my own past; for in his departure Gavin had taken with him my very identity, inseparable from our shared world and all its texture of memories; not recent and shared memories only, but the regions of my childhood, made over to him like a domain to its rightful heir after long absence returned. If ever by chance I was asked if I knew Gavin, I answered no, feeling this point-blank denial to be the mere truth. I might almost have given the same answer if I had been asked 'do you know Kathleen Raine', for all the country of imagination the poet had inhabited I had lost in losing Gavin; even 9 Paultons Square had become a house memory dared not enter. All that was left me was Ilford, in whose shameful heritage Gavin had no part; but also my learning. William Blake and the Neoplatonists were still, in the separation of our regions of imagination, incontestably my own, lending their dignity to my destitution. Many women whose loss has been as great have had less with which to spin their nettle-yarn.

*

When a bird can no longer fly on that invisible beam which guides it to its own place, because that place is gone, it must circle, unable to alight, inner and outer reality no longer congruous. I travelled far afield, to America, to Greece, to Italy, as if moving in outer space, on and on with no centre to draw me back. Since this is a record of inner experience I shall not describe these journeys which so mercifully distracted me, by day, from the far other journeyings of my nights. I began to write this record because I could not relinquish the life I could no longer live. Driven from the living reality I had to rebuild my world, memory by memory, or I had nothing; that is the truth of it, so far as I know it— I must live still in my love's house or I could not live at all. So much beauty how could I see lost? For my life—not because mine but because a life—seemed to me to have been something of infinite value, infinite meaning. Everything was there, if I could only discover what. Yet at the same time I needed to be rid of it, to free myself of myself. In giving birth is the motive to rid the body of an intolerable burden or to give life? Motives and intentions have no place in the hidden will that determines the processes of life. Useless to ask the spinners and weavers and builders of shells and nests and webs and combs why they must do what they do—why sea-molluscs must add lamina after lamina to the rim of some iridescent geometric shell they themselves are without sense to perceive. The law which decrees those shells neither begins nor ends with these blind labourers, inseparable from the single whole of nature. Like them we may have to labour at tasks of consciousness, whose shining structures are visible to spirits of an order as remote from us as we from the toilers between the tides.

Once, some months after his marriage, I met Gavin by chance outside the chemist's shop on the corner of Beaufort Street, by the traffic-lights. Meeting so, for the duration of a heart-beat, I was back in life. He kissed me, for all the world as if we had been the people we formerly were; it seemed natural to meet, to exchange those daily small things friends communicate because a relationship is continuous: except for one thing, that the moment was a fragment from a world which no longer existed. Like the sensation of an amputated limb, that irresolvable discord of joy and pain bore no relation to present reality.

For in the end of my relationship with Gavin was a finality I recognized as being altogether different in kind from anything I had ever known; I did not hope for anything more of life, not from hopelessness but because I neither desired nor needed anything more; I knew that my fate was, in the most profound sense, completed, that more would be superfluous; I can only put it so. If anyone had attempted to console me by saying that I might perhaps love again, or find some other thing, I would not have disbelieved them from despair but from a kind of plenitude; life could give me no more, for there was nothing more I could ever need or want. There was work to be done, but the work of the daimon; death I still must face, but death is not, perhaps, to me serious as an issue—my greatest fear is that it should come before my work is finished. I was, in any case, almost an old woman: what had I to lose but a few years? To relinquish the future is nothing when the thing loved is in the past.

Nothing remained but to write. I wrote the first draft of my story in Helen Sutherland's house, soon after my return from Washington; carried my volume to Italy, where as the guest of Hubert and Lelia Howard, I worked in the earthly paradise of Ninfa; continued work on the island of Euboea, looking from Philip Sherrard's white house to Parnassus and Helicon across the sound where the Argonauts sailed, and where now Gavin's brother's yacht floated at its moorings below; a spar from the wreck of my world. I carried it to Canna, where the Cuillin, whose jagged leaping summit had, from Sandaig, lain to the west, lay now in the wake of the ship's path, to the east, a mirage bright in the declining sun. 'Those infinite mountains of light' which had once been the Wannies, and once again the hills of Skye.

Last night I dreamed a weary dream
Beyond the Isle of Skye.

There are times and places when the outer world seems perfectly to image the inner, to reflect back to us, by 'correspondence', meanings, metaphysical intuitions. Perhaps it does so always, no less than when it gives back to us chaos for chaos, opacity for opacity, than when all is clear as in Boehme's 'vegetable glass' of wonders. Because love had made all there sacramental, or because of the clarity of that glass, I still found, in the Western Highlands, forms that answered my imagination. There is a natural symbol of peculiar beauty which meets us wherever the sun rises or sets over water: that track of light which travels from the sun to the place we stand. For each there is a path always silently at our feet, summoning us to walk over the water. In Greece I used to swim out along that track until the great ball of blood the setting sun there resembles dropped behind Mount Parnassus. In the Hebrides it is said that the newly dead leave the land and travel towards the west; do they then walk that track of liquid gold which seems at times to turn the water of the sea to light? Nowhere on earth does the summoning path shine with such splendour; but west of the Hebrides lies the edge of the world. Looking in imagination along the ever-present ever-summoning way, I could not yet follow it; the centre that drew me was still the rowan-tree of Sandaig, on the landward side, *terra firma*. I was not ready to take the way of no return, to go with that great fire of light on its night-journey.

*

If I here say little of the friends who received me, in my exile, into their houses, it is because the interchange of ideas, the sharing of impressions and knowledge, the laughter, the conversations, all these pleasant things belong to an impersonal order on the far side of the personal fate of which this book is the record.

All these sanctuaries of my friends' houses have in

common one thing: all are dedicated, almost, it might be said, consecrated, as monastic houses are ('at least in principle', as Marco Pallis would say) to something besides personal ends. Margaret Campbell told me, when first I was her guest at Canna House, of the prayer she had made that all who came to the isle should receive its blessing. She and John Lorne Campbell are converts to the Catholic faith, 'the auld religion', strongest of many bonds with the people of the Isles living and dead. Hubert and Lelia Howard, latest and perhaps last custodians of the diminished but still great estates of the dukes of Sermoneta (Lelia's inheritance) regard that feudal task as a sacred trust; something no longer imaginable in a profane world which seeks to possess absolutely, and not, as in the older civilization, 'under God'. The planting of orchards and crops and trees, the restoration of the castle of Sermoneta as a summer-school for young musicians (selling pieces of land to restore equivalent pieces of the ancient roof, or to build bathrooms and students' cubicles into the great keeps like honey-comb into an ancient tree) are works undertaken within the framework of the Christian *civitas dei*. There was truth (the historian's tag notwithstanding) in the concept of a Christian Roman empire to whose holiness the works of her artificers bear witness. Is not civilization, as such, the empire of the human imagination, of that in man which is precisely not determined by economic pressures and the instincts of the *bête humaine*? Who, in the city well-named eternal, since so much of eternity is reflected in its works of three successive civilizations, can fail to be aware of this? Art is the city of the soul. Hubert and Lelia Howard, like those painted donors whose grave intelligent faces look up at some golden vision of virgin and angels, still served that holy city as their ancestors had done in unbroken succession since Aeneas founded his colony.

I was given, on my last visit to Ninfa, the room which had belonged to Marguerite Caetani, the last duchess patron of poets, whose magazines *Commerce* and *Botteghe Obscure* made literary history. Alexis Léger had written for *Commerce*. How could I, writing at her table, forget that what I write must abide the judgement of civilization, of that unbroken tradition carried into my own present by T. S. Eliot (her cousin) and her friends Alexis Léger and Valéry? Now that I had gained admission to that company, I saw with shame how I had neglected the work of the poet through personal unhappiness (and personal happiness also, though less often) forgetting that these are, in the light of eternity, only the furnaces in which natural experience is transmuted into those unageing forms.

Two especially, among Rome's treasures of the imagination, put me to shame. The first was that dungeon of San Pietro ad Vinculam where the barbarian chieftains conquered in battle were kept alive until such time as some general should arrive in Rome to hold his Triumph; they were decapitated at the end of the show. The long list of their names is there; and with them those of the Apostles Peter and Paul; obscure figures in such company. It was St. Paul whose spirit spoke to me, that slight, indomitable Jew. writing (a stone's throw from the not dissimilar prison of the Christians' fellow-victims, the lions) to his friends to pray, not for his release, but 'that God would open unto us a door of utterance, to speak the mystery of Christ'.

In the city which itself embodies all the dreams and visions of the Christian cult, that dungeon, unadorned as a coal-hole, most deeply moved me just because it preceded all embodiment. One could not get nearer than this to the source of Christendom. St. Paul could not have known that his Christ would rule in the city of the Emperors, nor that his own letters would be read throughout a civilization which did not then exist, and which came into existence solely through the triumph of imagination over power, and over the *bête humaine*. He, unlike those tragic and romantic chieftains was free in his bonds (you can see the stone to which they were tied) and in his death beyond the reach of the executioners, who have no power over the

113

kingdom not of this world. I then began to understand why freedom is to be found only in the lion's mouth; not only because every lesser kind must assuredly be lost, since this world in its very nature imperils all, takes all in the end; but because only untrammelled by hopes and fears can we contemplate existence as it appears to the one mind within whose unity our wholes are parts; fear blinds us to the glory of many 'portions of eternity too great for the eye of man'. The martyrs, courting that death, had aspired to total freedom; not to death as such, not a death-wish. No civilization was ever founded on a death-wish.

Hubert Howard took me, one afternoon in a downpour of rain, to visit the Keats museum. The room where Keats died is a little larger than the dungeon of the barbarian kings and Christian apostles, and much more beautiful, with its painted rafters and view of the Spanish steps; a fitting room for the poet to die in who had perceived the truth of beauty. We were shown the treasures by the custodian and his wife; and I must have said to Hubert something about Keats and Shelley (who in the great company of Rome seemed diminished to the stature of friends and members of one's own family) being over-shadowed by those greater legislators of the world who (in their lifetimes more unacknowledged than any poet) had created Christendom. Hubert, deeply Catholic though he is in faith and by family tradition, replied, 'but they too gave all they had'. It seemed to me then that all the enduring works and living memories of the Eternal City are sacrifices which the gods to whom they were made have accepted because of their purity.

I returned from Italy by way of Corsica, exchanging the austere sweet grandeur of the Palazzo Caetani for Homer's land of the Laestrygonians, those cannibals who attacked Odysseus and his mariners (coasting from Polyphemus' cave below the Cyclopian city of Norma, on the hill behind Ninfa and its fountains) with showers of sling-stones. I went there to visit Frederica Rose who (herself a Laestrygonian by affinity, a General's daughter whose early passion was reckless hunting) had found in Corsica, where she had lived for many years, the counterpart of her own nature. (She was the first to light upon those carved menhirs of Filitosa, seen one way archaic warriors armed with swords, seen the other, uncompromisingly phallic). Here I felt myself more remote from all familiar land-marks than in any place I have ever been. Greece I seemed to have known always, as if in some former life I had been native there. Of the Italy of art, all civilized Europeans are in some degree citizens; but until I set foot on the harbour of Bastia (Balzac, that admirer of Napoleon, I found, had been there before me, however) Corsica had had no existence for me at all, real or imaginary. As if rising into existence for the first time, therefore, I watched the unfolding panorama of those savage snow-jagged alps, those deep romantic chasms hung with chest-nut-forests, those Laestrygonian bastions of Calvi, the citadel of Sartène perched like the Tibetan Potala on its rock. The luxuriant olive-trees, the *maquis* whose lentisk and arbutus (on the dry mountains of Greece barely waist-high) forms a dense and fragrant woodland of evergreen filled with blackbird-song, rose before me unsullied by any hopes or fears of mine, memories or anticipations. From Bastia to Calvi we travelled in a little *michelin* train on a railway-track which suggested, in the smallness of its scale in relaton to that vertiginous and rugged scenery, a 00-gauge model railway, for ever taking hairpin-bends round precipices, plunging into tunnels hewn through the clean rock, often with goats or cattle running along the track in front of us. The autumn moon which travelled with us seemed to be plunging down into gorges, or suddenly reappearing high overhead, now in front, now behind; unfolding, as in a dream, the savage and enchanted interior landscape of Kubla Khan. Our fellow-travellers, women with bulging baskets, men with guns, were speaking the Corsican lan-guage, defence of their race against the encroachments of successive civilizations whose remains (Graeco-Roman,

Genoese, French Imperial) seem so strangely alien, as if shipwrecked on the rocks and submerged reefs of an indomitable barbarism. I listened to that tongue, never spoken by civilized man or woman, wondering what unguessed meanings and modes of feeling and being, incommunicable except in that speech, were preserved, by those archaic wards, in the consciousness of the living; attitudes and thoughts of the Læstrygonians and the builders of megaliths.

At one point there had been a landslide on the line, and we all had to get out, carrying our baggage through the freshly fallen rock and earth, to where the other *michelin*, from the Calvi side, was waiting to take us on. The episode, slight in itself, reappeared later in a dream, from which I wrote a poem; but the dream's symbolic content must have come less from the impact of Corsican scenery (to me that island was and remains a place of impenetrable strangeness) but from my conversations with Frederica. In that relentless isle she had worked out her salvation, returning, after years in the wilderness, to the Church; (of England, at that, true to her native Gloucestershire). I had known her first as a Marxist, an elegant and gallant traitor to her own traditions; and now, after adventures which in risk and action rivalled Conrad, in romantic dedication to love *jusqu' au bout* some film of Greta Garbo (or was it Marlene Dietrich who on such well-bred naked feet walked her knife-edge of burning desert after some irretrievable *légionnaire*?). She had found, at the end of it all, that to which all loves, even the most deluded, lead in the end: one can but say, God. ('Call it X,' I tried saying to Ivor Richards once, hesitating to use a word, like its only Scriptural equation, too often abused. 'No, no, you have to say God, there is no synonym'—and the author of Basic English, if anyone, should know.) 'At least she knew where she wanted to get to,' Frederica said, as she closed the book of saints in which we had looked up the story of how St. Mary of Egypt had worked her passage to Jerusalem as a prostitute. She believed in the miraculous, having made a vow to pray in

116

every church in Corsica for the salvation of some incorrigible lover, and she had, in a sudden illumination, realized that the grace she had asked for him, was offered likewise to herself: a thing that seldom occurs to women in love, set only upon drawing up the beloved out of the depths.

Hubert Howard, on whose ancestral tree hang popes and Catholic martyrs like golden apples among the emperors and earls, had not once said to me 'go back to the Church'; it was Frederica, who had been, in her own words, 'scraped across the stony bed of the universe', who said go back, accept the divine forgiveness offered to all.

In part I clung to my remorse because that last painful strand still bound my life to Gavin; in part because I feared to entrust myself, yet again, to hope, for fear of being once more dashed down. Yet I knew she was right, it was time to relinquish personal hopes and fears. That confrontation must have been decisive; for when I dreamed of stepping out of a train that had come to a halt among high wild mountains, I knew the dream was a symbol of freedom; a state which, as I began slowly to enter upon it, seemed of a quality scarcely discernible, like air. No longer to be impelled or compelled by desire or fear was, in that dream, like getting out of the train at Penrith with my children in October 1940, and smelling, in the darkness, the forgotten scent of hills and sheep.

*

Those who enter a religious order, who leave, as it is said, the world, take a new name; and this represents a truth; for the former human personality is (at least in principle, and in many instances in reality) left behind. Life, from this time on, is no longer lived in terms of the human ego, its desires and hopes and fears; another principle takes over, and the new man or woman has become an instrument of

117

another principle. St. Paul's 'not I, but Christ liveth in me' is not an exclamation of emotion, but an exact expression of that new mode of life; which can only begin when the renunciation of the personal existence is absolute. I had now reached this threshold, reached an understanding, at least, of what was now demanded of me; understood, too, not without anguish, that no renunciation less than absolute is a renunciation at all, but a mere bargaining for the thing most desired at the price of everything else. My life had hitherto been a series of such gambler's losses; but now if I could not place myself beyond these hopes and despairs. I could not go on. I knew enough of the literature of the Perennial Philosophy to know at what parting of the ways I stood; and, confronted with a choice I had hoped never to have to make, knew that others had made it, that the way of absolute renunciation of hopes and fears and desires had a thousand times been found to be the way of freedom; the terrible words 'he that loseth his life, the same shall find it' met me. But still I could not turn away from the past, which seemed to contain all the treasure of my life, to enter the emptiness of—not an unknown future, for of the future I neither asked nor expected anything—but of a new mode of being altogether, a futureless condition which is nevertheless freedom itself, as such; that poverty, or emptiness, of whose great joy many have told, but all saying that the price to be paid is the relinquishment of the hopes and fears of which natural life is an incessant flow. I sheltered myself in the last tatters of my egoism, remorse. And if, besides, I argued with myself, catastrophe had followed my most sincere attempt to perfect even one relationship, had I not better keep away from the gods altogether, as dangerous destroyers? I refused to draw the obvious conclusion, that since what had happened was what had to happen, given all the circumstances, it therefore was, (as all reality can only be) the expression of the divine will, terrible to me and to Gavin only insofar as the judgement passed upon us was not what either would have wished. But at every moment, that Judgement is passed in the inexorable terms of reality itself; there are no mistakes.

Those patterns of lives Plato's Er saw spread out for the souls to choose were varied, better and worse, good and bad; and so it is in Indian and Tibetan accounts of incarnation and reincarnation; but all say that good and bad alike must be discarded by the souls who seek for freedom; for all those patterns are but variations on a single theme, the suffering consequent upon all that has in time its beginning, middle and end, birth and death, rise and decline. What are the typically fated people, Oedipus and Macbeth, Deirdre, or Balzac's Rafael de Valentin, but the doers and sufferers of calamity? Saints, sages, musicians like Mozart, seem to enter the world already free, knowing more than experience can ever teach those who struggle through its toils. Blake knew that knowledge belongs to the state of innocence, and his annals of experience are all the devious wanderings of ignorance in 'Satan's labyrinth'. I can now myself say that I have learned nothing from experience, from my mistakes, from trial and error, or from the mere passage of time: only through rifts in these clouds, as if from another order of knowledge altogether. Tragedies, after all, however nobly enacted and grandly endured, are, as seen by wisdom, the storms of illusion, the webs woven in ignorance and passion by those who 'do but slenderly know themselves'. In tragedy we can finally admire only the grandeur of humanity's never-abandoned struggle to attain the moment of transcendence; without which there can be no catharsis, no liberation. Having myself at last perhaps emerged, stunned and exhausted and too late, only what lies on the far side of that moment seems now to matter. The term of all the devious roads lives are is another condition of being altogether, known only to those who have experienced it; who are perhaps more numerous than profane literature might lead one to suppose. The people in the cave may pity as 'disillusioned' those others who no longer care for the shadow-prizes nor

119

compete for them. But the loss of illusion, for Plato as for the followers of the Buddhist or any other *way* of enlightenment, is known to be the threshold of that state of being which is its own joy.

*

The Light of Common Day

IF ANY reader has read thus far perhaps such a one will ask how I could have lived my life with my head in the clouds, so unaware of the world around me. Yet if I have written my story upon the assumption that mental things are real and constantly act as the causes of events, operating through thought no less than through physical action, it can hardly be said that the belief makes life easier; on the contrary, for the sins of the heart are agents. So indeed is the heart's love and goodness, but my attempts at these can scarcely be called successful. However, if my attempts to live 'up to' my view of reality have failed, I have not, either, spared myself its inevitable judgement.

If I have written, then, of an inner world and its events it is not because I have had no occasion to notice the outer world, as this appears to a society indoctrinated with the notion that the material level is all. That level has its virtues too—feeding the hungry, tending the sick, prolonging physical existence, and the many other social virtues of our society. Sexual 'permissiveness' also might seem from the point of view of materialism a social advance; and Platonic love would be meaningless in materialist terms. It may be said that my own adventure into such a relationship will hardly commend it. But if I cannot defend my failure I can at least defend my values because I believe these inevitably follow from the real nature of things. If the mental world is a world of causes; if man is not only an animal, but also a soul and a spirit, then the issues I so terribly encountered cannot be evaded. In this life, or after this life (so I believe) every one of us must encounter that reality.

121

By the logic of circumstances, no doubt, one of those far-off figures of the Cambridge of my student years whose falsehoods had so bedevilled me, reappeared for a moment. I remembered her face as one I had seen; perhaps at the Heretics, those Sunday evening meetings which it had been 'advanced' to attend in that world now so remote both in time and in more important respects; or perhaps her face only resembled other faces bearing the imprint of the same ideology. How easily, in those days, had I been put out of countenance when one of those bright clever 'emancipated' faces had happened to focus on me (such people always look you straight in the face, seeing no reason to respect the privacy or mystery of another being) with 'I'm afraid I don't understand what you mean by the word "beauty' "—or whatever it might be. They didn't of course; but what was implied was that there was no such thing. It was always some qualitative word that such people met with some unanswerable negation based upon the premiss that only the quantifiable is 'real'. As a schoolgirl I had lacked both the knowledge and the courage to defend Keats's 'beauty is truth, truth beauty' against the reduction of man, nature and works of art to material terms (human will to animal instinct, animal instinct to chemistry, and so on down). I had not taken the measure of their ignorance; had not realized that I was confronting people who had not (for example) the sense of the holy, or of intellectual beauty, and who were not therefore in a position to compare these qualities with their own quantitative standards. How certain people come to represent materialist ideologies can, for the present argument, be disregarded; for whatever reason many people do so; 'for we wrestle not against flesh and blood' but against ideologies and power-structures and wickedness in high places. And those high places cannot be written off as 'fascist dictatorships' and 'juntas' and 'colonels', but concern us far more nearly, in the 'mass media', the Universities, and among the well-meaning when these are governed by false values.

122

Confronted with a mind which had so remarkably retained the stamp and style of the twenties, I knew with shame that I was in the presence of a mental deformity I had myself once been in haste to assume, and which I had allowed to plunge me into the loveless inhuman courses of my early years. As, for example, by way of conversation on psychiatry, I said that as I did not believe the Freudian doctrine to be true I was mistrustful of psychoanalysis; and she replied that she was far from being a 'strict' Freudian herself: 'An elderly spinster, for instance, for whom it is *too late* is much better left with her sublimations.' To such a statement there is no answer given the premiss: that that for which it may be 'too late' (the sexual act) is self-evidently a greater good than 'sublimations', which include in effect religion and all the arts, besides such lesser pleasures as gardening, keeping a cat or a dog, indeed practically all human activities not directly or indirectly concerned with the survival and reproduction of the physical body.

Yet she spoke without any trace of irony and in perfect good humour; without the saving bitterness of the 'double-take' such an utterance might have implied. The tone was, rather, conciliatory; meeting me half way, as if here at least two women who shared a Cambridge background could meet in agreement. Her remark was made, besides, with the assurance with which only received opinion is repeated; there was no question in 1965, as there might have been in 1925, of an 'advanced', daring or controversial statement. In behaviourist circles the remark would have passed as no more strange than a platitude upon the weather; and yet the question begged nothing less than Job's and Oedipus' and Blake's question, 'What is man?'

Perhaps Freud, a civilized man, was being paradoxical when he wrote of all the arts as mis-directed sexual libido; not so much mis-directed, he probably said, as re-directed. But the fact remains that Jung, who knew him well (and honoured him, as all must, as the first to chart the landfall of that great unexplored mental continent, 'the un-

123

conscious') parted with him on precisely that issue. There are, besides, plenty of people who so understand him and see nothing unacceptable in a theory whose strict and literal application must lead to a reversion of man to the human animal. It is not for me to point the moral of Poe's story of the lunatic asylum whose inmates locked up the sane men and conducted the establishment on their own lines. The 'cure', these days, is so often worse than the disease; and to remove from a human soul its conflicts and its suffering may be more kill than cure.

This person and I had on another occasion a conversation still more astonishing. She spoke of a medical colleague who 'specialized' in homosexuality. 'Is he successful?' I asked. 'Oh, yes—but of course it is easier to graft a vagina on a man than a penis on a woman;' (or it may have been the other way round). Again there was nothing to be said; I wonder what the author of the *Phaedrus* would have thought; though the joke might have appealed to Aristophanes, whose spherical proto-lovers were certainly anatomical oddities. Yet given the behaviourist (premiss that love is the rubbing together of little fleshy appendages) the rest follows. What other felicity, what other view of love, homosexual or otherwise, have those to offer who deny the soul? I thought with affection of that great Catholic sinner the Baron de Charlus who in Charlie Morel beheld (rightly or wrongly or both) the Archangel Michael. . . . '*Quand le monde moderne avilit,*' Péguy wrote, '*mettons que c'est alors qu'il travaille de sa partie.*'

It seemed to me that the Utopias of atheism may well be the hells of the spirit; and the sexual orgasm itself, emptied of the spiritual dimension which makes of marriage a Christian sacrament, and the act of sex in both Buddhist and Hindu iconography a symbol of the eternal generation of the world by God, one of the torments of those hells.

A more famous and austere atheist is said to have said that sex should be as simple a matter as drinking a glass of water. Against Lenin's colourless odourless and tasteless draught I set that cup of water given 'for my sake'; and those six water-pots at the wedding-feast whose transmutation was the first evidence of the presence in Galilee of the divine principle. The gods are forever turning water into wine, drawing milk and honey from springs and fountains, offering another kind of bread than that made from stones; only they can. Materialism reverses the process.

I might have pitied her ignorance had I not been unforgiving, not indeed of this merely conventional transmitter of current opinion, but of myself as I had been, who had allowed all that evil nonsense to corrupt my own youth. ('We do not cry because we are sorry' I remember parroting in those days, 'we are sorry because we cry.' How convenient that behaviourist maxim for an unkind daughter who could look on her mother's tears with indifference!)

Winifred Nicholson tells an anecdote of her great-grandmother, who was also Bertrand Russell's grandmother (that same Lady Stanley whose portrait looks down, still critical, upon the generations of Girton students) remarking, after a visit from her grandson, 'I don't know why it is that all my grandchildren are so *stupid*.' I don't know why she thought the great logician 'stupid' at that time; but the 'stupidity' of logical positivism lies, if anywhere, in its premises. Logicians never admit that their premises are open to question; perhaps do not know it. If it is true that the crassness of English philosophy (Yeats observed that the English have the poorest philosophic literature in the world) has lain always in the quality of its premises Lady Stanley may in this respect have been right about her grandson's 'stupidity'. Yet I no longer believe that these apparently impervious rationalists who demand so aggressively that we others should 'explain what you mean by. . . .' (God, love, beauty, the good, the soul, the Logos,) are always victims of what the Church calls 'invincible ignorance', that stupidity against which the gods themselves are said to struggle in vain. To judge others by myself I would guess that in many more it is the will that has at some time denied and rejected spiritual knowledge. In the choice of premisses the will is free: logic cannot dictate the ground from which its conclusions proceed; and I wonder whether the loveless beautyless state is not the cause rather than the effect of such systems? If, disregarding those superstructures so dazzling to ignorance, we regard their foundations, these will be seen for what they are. Blake never answered Urizen's arguments, but merely drew his portrait.

Premisses, I suppose the positivists would argue, are necessarily simple sense-experiences of physical objects, 'positive', like the kitchen table Virginia Woolf took as her primary philosophical solid. But is even the kitchen table only what it seems to so limited an experience of reality as a quantitative philosophy allows? Is not that perhaps just the point? Science is forever boasting of knowing and discovering 'more' about the universe; but the only 'more' with which it is concerned is quantitative; why, then, should we look to science to tell us 'more' about the nature of the things it measures and describes? Going to the moon, or splitting the atom is only (Blake again) 'the same dull round', more of the same thing. But what if there were a qualitative 'more', of which we remain for the most part unaware?

Whatever 'nature-mysticism' may be it is not 'the pathetic fallacy', but a perception as 'positive' as barking one's shin on Virginia Woolf's kitchen table, or stubbing one's toe on Dr. Johnson's stone. My mother (who only when she had passed eighty began to talk with me of such things; but perhaps rather because of a readiness in me to listen than an impulse in her to break silence before it was too late) one day confided to me an experience which, as she said, she had told no one; even though it came to her before she was eighteen. She was sitting on a moor among the heather, alone; 'and I saw that it was alive'; so she put it: that was all. 'I thought you would understand,' she said. As she spoke it seemed to me as if she, and I, had been the same person, our two lives lived by the same consciousness; for I knew what

126

she meant, I had seen my hyacinth as she had seen her heather moor. My father, to whom she had never told what she had seen, would have thought he understood; as would almost anyone who 'loves nature'. But what my mother had experienced was something quite different from Wordsworth's 'impulse from a vernal wood', nor was it, for her, a mere 'belief' (derived by Wordsworth at second-hand in all likelihood by way of Coleridge from Thomas Taylor's translation of Plotinus *On Felicity*) that 'every flower enjoys the air it breathes'. Plotinus had known, as my mother knew, from immediate perception; his premiss (like that of Moses who saw the bush 'burning'), was *positive*; but such premisses cannot be 'explained' to stupid clever people. The objects of perception are the same yet not the same; the object of knowledge is itself different; the difference lies not in what is known 'about' it, but in the thing known. It is possible to perceive more, or less, of what is there, in a sense immeasurable in terms of quantity. It is not the logic of the materialists which precludes this knowledge, but a kind of consciousness; and to their 'I don't understand what you mean by . . .' one can but quote Blake, 'Reason, or the ratio of what we have already known, is not the same as it shall be when we know more.' It is just in these primary experiences that the difference lies; the mystic and the positivist do not see different things; neither do they see the same things and draw different conclusions; they see the same things, but differently.

For certain kinds of knowledge (my mother's vision of the moor as 'alive', or my own hyacinth) once is enough. Those who have had the experience recognize instantly what is meant by others who speak of it; those who have not can never argue it away by logic, or dissect it by science. The terrible thing is that spiritual realities should have ceased to be premisses. I would despair were it not for the irreversible nature of knowledge; we may come to know but we cannot un-know. Those who have reached a certain degree of understanding do not lose the way any more; as

127

Plato assures us in the *Phaedrus*, for those who have once trodden the upper path it is not ordained that they shall ever again tread the lower one.

*

Emerging from my ten years' work on Blake, from my years with Gavin engaged in what was, though the part I had played may have been played amiss, a spiritual drama, I realized that I was engaged in a great battle now being fought in the world: my own story took its place within a much wider context. The battlefield was upon me; but where, now, were the strongholds against the ever-rising tide?

I took my father (he had always loved the theatre) to the first production of Osborne's *Look Back in Anger*. He was incredulous and indignant. Why could not that young fellow, who had had the advantage (in my father's boyhood given to few) of a university education, have set himself to work for the good of society? Teaching, for example—then his ill-nature would have evaporated (as ill-nature always does) as an unacknowledged state of being (rightly) ashamed of himself gave place to the satisfaction of work well done? My father, his years of work behind him, had no sympathy for the self-pity of Jimmy Porter. My father's life had been a life of work well done; the modern 'left' with its endless demand for 'rights', with its ever-diminishing sense of duty, puzzled and distressed him. My father's kind had not wished to disrupt, and to air their grievances, but to reform, to extend the Good and the Best to more people, in theory to everybody; for my father would never have admitted that Shakespeare and Wordsworth and Euclid, and above all Jesus Christ, could be less than universal in their humanity. 'We needs must love the highest when we see it' was one of those too glibly repeated maxims in which he felt that much wisdom was summarized. My father's generation of Christian socialists had been Blake's 'golden builders' of the New Jerusalem, the city 'coming down from heaven'. He could

128

see no other socialism than that of the kingdom of Christ on earth. But if my father refused to admit that the new subversive socialism, and even communism itself, is inseparable from its root in atheist materialism, I, living a generation later, could not fail to see that this was so. In that philosophy all the legion manifestations of the nihil have their common ground. There has been much talk of the 'two cultures' as if this were a simple opposition of 'arts' against 'sciences' or a political matter; but the issue, under every guise, is between atheist humanism and the *sophia perennis*. For my father Christianity was the religion of the poor, of the slaves and the dispossessed who were those 'early Christians' whose catacombs were not unlike the coal-mines of his own County Durham Methodist people. A godless proletariat was, for him, the most bitter disillusionment; but history is unanswerable.

Not so much the phenomena in themselves ('Conduct and work grow coarse, and coarse the soul') struck fear into me, but what lay behind. Some instinct told me to re-read *The Possessed*; which when I first read it had seemed to me (under Western eyes) an almost incredible account of the triumph of nihilism over social order and human dignity; but then Russia was a 'backward' country where things were possible which could not happen in our more civilized society. Now it seemed like a commentary upon England in the 1960s: 'Do you know that we are tremendously powerful already? Our party does not consist only of those who commit murder and arson, fire off pistols in the traditional fashion, or bite colonels. They are only a hindrance. . . . Listen, I've reckoned them all up: a teacher who laughs with children at their God and at their cradle is on our side. The lawyer who defends an educated murderer because he is more cultured than his victims and could not help murdering them to get money is one of us. The schoolboys who murder a peasant for the sake of sensation are ours. The juries who acquit every criminal are ours. The prosecutor who trembles at a trial for fear he should not

129

seem advanced enough is ours. Among officials and literary men we have lots, lots, and they don't know it themselves.... When I left Russia, Littre's dictum that crime is insanity was all the rage; I come back and I find that crime is no longer insanity, but simply common sense, almost a duty; anyway, a gallant protest.'

I felt myself impelled to rally to some standard; but where discover a sanctuary and custodian of the spiritual values threatened in a world whose purpose to destroy was becoming increasingly undisguised, but in the Church? I began to attend Mass on Sunday mornings, as the strongest political protest I was able to make; in sheer contempt of the slip-shod lie-about newspaper-reading English atheist Sunday morning I went at 8 a.m.; there is something cleansing in the mere discipline of early-rising; the arriving at a certain place at a certain time sets a form upon the day. Near the back of the Church of the Holy Redeemer I would sit where I could look at the photograph of the face of the Holy Shroud which hangs in a small side-chapel. Far other faces were illustrated on the pages of those Sunday newspapers which lay still unopened on the doorsteps of Paultons Square along with the milk bottles (since even atheist man does not live by bread alone—better perhaps if he did) as I returned from Mass. I do not read the Sunday newspapers; but those who do so might, so I felt, judge world affairs more truly in the light of that daily-enacted symbolic restoration. I began to feel that I ought to return to the Church. All very well for me, who had read Proclus and the Upanishads; but if I, over the years, had become learned in the literature of spiritual knowledge, for the unlearned only the Christian religion makes accessible that knowledge, and a way of life consistent with it.

I was, besides, ashamed of my lack of simplicity. In Cambridge one evening Frances Cornford had so put me to shame; I had been cavilling at this or that in the Christian religion, and she said, I remember, in her thrilling tragic voice, 'I only know that there I find water and I go to drink.'

But though I had often forced myself through church doors I never had found water there. Or perhaps I am one of those who cannot be made to drink.

Again, it was the politics of this world, rather than any inner impulse of assent, that drove me to conclude, once more, that in Western Europe Christianity alone stands (for all but the learned few) for the values of eternity. Kafka saw that 'Mankind can only become a gray, formless, and therefore nameless mass through a fall from the Law which gives it form. But in that case there is no above and below any more; life is levelled out to mere existence; there is no struggle, no drama, only the consumption of matter, decay.'; words now no longer a prophecy but the description of a grey formlessness everywhere present where current ideologies prevail.

Of all the teachers of my generation I am perhaps most indebted to Jung. At all events, I continue to be aware of the debt, when others are forgotten; for Jung points the way to a living access to the originals of which the myths and symbols of religion are formulations. If I have come to understand the power and depth of the Christian mythology, it is, I must confess, by way of study and experience, and not because these icons have ever moved me. It is true that the more I have come to know, both of life and of metaphysics, the greater my reverence for these symbols of the cult has become; but the cult has in no way moved me, the symbols have not lived for me, as the symbols of poetry have lived, or those mysteries unveiled, sometimes, in dreams. Jung is surely right in divining that at this time what was once encountered 'outside' must be encountered within the *psyche*, an interior world no longer, as perhaps once it was, inclined to project itself upon cult-images. I have read nearly all Jung's published works, some with greater interest, some with less, all with imaginative delight at the rediscovery of the lost kingdom of the gods. Yet I could never quite call him master; in his *Answer to Job* 'God', by a sleight-of-hand, is made to appear as something less than

131

Job, something man is 'enduring' within himself. Martin Buber (it was Louis MacNeice who first told me to read *I and Thou*, and David Gascoyne re-read that seminal book repeatedly) never compromised the vision of the divine transcendence which is the glory of the ancient Hebrew poem; nor Kafka either.

I had myself made a study of certain traditional myths in the course of my Blake work (Cupid and Psyche, the Two Goddesses, Narcissus, and other themes relating to the descent and return of souls) and I discovered in the course of my work a number of Jungian re-interpretations to be (assuming the meaning of the myths to be those understood by the cultures which created and made use of them) in the simple academic sense, incorrect; but also less far-reaching, less subtle, less poetically and philosophically amenable, than the interpretations of Porphyry and Plotinus, Proclus and Sallust, and that central mainstream of imaginative learning which flows in unbroken continuity from Orpheus to Ovid, carrying a perpetual renaissance from the Florentine school into all poetic traditions, continuous throughout English poetry down to the poets of Yeats's Ireland. I had discovered that knowledge of myths is a kind of learning not to be had in a day; and having in this field myself become passably literate, could see in even Jungian psychologists a tendency to rush in with the inadequate interpretations of an insufficient learning. For the psychologists are in truth newcomers in the great field of symbolic thought and discourse. They are inclined to forget—or, rather, have not yet discovered—that mythology is a language inseparable from the metaphysics of the Perennial Philosophy, whose expression it is.

René Guénon's bitter diatribes and intellectual pride suited my mood, and his masterly discourse on the metaphysical aspect of traditional symbols commanded my respect. Coomaraswamy's books on the aesthetics of the *philosophia perennis* I already knew. On Philip Sherrard's introduction I went to see Marco Pallis, the *éminence grise* of

132

that school in England, himself a Buddhist, who had studied in the monasteries of Tibet, and a friend and correspondent of Frithjof Schuon, and others of the school of Tradition. Where, I asked Marco, could we turn?

Any one of the 'revealed' traditions, he said, might be followed; all were valid 'ways'; the essential thing was to adhere wholly to one, and to avoid eclecticism, since each is in itself a whole whose parts are not separable from that totality. One may, according to circumstances (which include personal sympathies and dispathies) follow any one of these Ways. Very occasionally highly gifted souls may be able to dispense with these traditional forms; but none can deny their adequacy. One must, besides, participate in a living tradition; the Pythagorean and neo-Platonic learning is a dead language, for the Mysteries of the ancient world are no longer practised. So there I was back again at the point from which I had hoped to escape; I said I supposed, then, that he advised me to return to the Catholic church. 'I did not say anything of the kind,' Marco would say, with his super-subtle Greek smile, 'I merely stated the arguments.' He, like myself, did not 'like' Christianity, and found himself, even though born in the Greek Orthodox world, out of sympathy with it—'but that is not to deny its validity', he would hasten to add. He himself having lived in India and travelled in Tibet, had a pretext, so to say, for choosing Buddhism. I wished I could think of any pretext for following Vendanta; but I knew that to do so would, in my own case, be mere exoticism.

I don't know what I had expected or hoped for; what unimagined, unimaginable enlightenment. And do not, Marco said, suppose that the Eastern religions are less in decadence than is Christianity; so near the end of the *kali yuga* all means fail. 'But so long as I am myself alive,' he added, 'Buddhism will continue to exist.' Surely there are Christians who still keep the Church open as a spiritual channel? How could I doubt this? And yet, and yet.

I am doubtless in closer sympathy with Marco's school
133

than with any other; had I not, in discovering the secret of Blake's 'originality' found it to lie precisely in his fidelity to these origins and originals? But even with these initiates of wisdom I could not wholly identify myself.

Not one of the principal exponents of that school was in fact living within the tradition to which they themselves were native. Coomaraswamy, praising Hinduism, was educated in England and lived his adult life in America. Of all their writings, those of Schuon most illuminate Christianity, but their author is a Moslem convert. Several members of the group are, as was Guénon himself, Moslems; Marco, born into a Greek Orthodox family, a Buddhist. Were they not all, under the disguise of strict adherence to tradition, in fact refugees, or rebels, and by the very assumption of Islam, or Makayana Buddhism, as the case might be, changing the nature of the tradition assumed? Even while denouncing the confusion of the different traditions, were they not all carried on an interfusing tide? How could Marco's Buddhism not be coloured by Greek Orthodox Christianity? Or Philip Sherrard's Greek Orthodoxy by his Bloomsbury background and his training as a Cambridge historian? Was not Guénon's Islam that of an embittered French intellectual? Eclecticism, whether or not desirable, is in practice unavoidable, its implicit syncretism may even be the best contribution of this school. If I were to try once again to make a Catholic of myself, only what I had learned from Indian and Platonic sources could make that return tolerable.

My second doubt was whether these defenders of the ancient springs would recognize the 'wind that blows where it listeth. We hear the sound thereof, and it is gone.' The parable of the new wine in old bottles might, I felt, be applied to the school of Guénon. Forms will always be new. These people, I sensed, did not live by the imagination; was there, even, a certain hatred, or envy of the creative spirit in the monotonously negative judgements passed (for example) upon Jung and Teilhard de Chardin who, whatever their limitations, are seminal imaginative thinkers? God knows I myself was sick of the cant of progress and evolution, most often heard in those quarters where spiritual, intellectual and moral retrogression is most evident; and inherently probable as I felt the opposite view to be (the decline towards an Armageddon) a view supported not least by the very evidence of 'progress' the evolutionists point to with most confidence and pride, yet I could not relinquish my poet's faith in the prophetic spirit, which has never failed.

Nor am I convinced that the neo-Platonic tradition is no longer viable. Marco might say that the Eleusinian Mysteries were, like the Mass, kept alive not by the imagination but by the informing gods; but in Plato's Garden of the Muses (call it Jung's world of the archetypes, or Yeats's and Edwin Muir's *anima mundi*), poets may still find the living immortal presences, whether like Keats or Hölderlin they name the gods by their old names, or like Blake re-clothe them in the dress of the present. Are poets initiated not in an apostolic but in a poetic succession, still held in the chain of magnetized rings of which Plato spoke? Perhaps the springs and fountains are now only a thin trickle; but can I not say of my tradition, as Marco of the Buddhism of a Tibet which in 1965 no longer exists, so long as I live the poetic transmission shall not die?

*

If the One Consciousness is now seeking some other form than a 'Church' (and Jung too saw with dismay, in that mind, such a change of mode,) it is not that the reality to be communicated is other than it was and forever is; the new mode seems rather a change in our manner of receiving than in what is to be received. 'A church in the hearts of men,' Gay Taylor was told in a dream. It is as if the informing presences have abandoned their old habitations, the cult-images, and once more

 . . . the chill marble seems to sweat
    While each peculiar power forgoes his wonted seat.
135

Only now it is the Christian Saints who are departing from their shrines. We must, it seems, now meet the gods on other ground; in the psyche, as Jung affirmed. 'Reality' cannot be defined, but only experienced; and if for other ages reality took up its abode in cult images and liturgy, for ours it is not so; if we meet the gods it is within. Having there (in dream or vision) beheld them, we may see plainly enough that the cult-images are their true portraits; but there must be others like myself who have recognized the truth of these aids and props of faith only retrospectively having come to the reality otherwise; they do not evoke for us, as for earlier Christian centuries, the realities they embody. However we may assent to the truth of these old depictions, it is no longer through them we receive that which they depict; they are no longer icons, but pictures; imperceptibly the walls where they hang have ceased to be the walls of churches and have become the walls of museums.

That reality, as such, is not bound by any of those forms which may at one time or another embody it is self-evident to any Hindu or Buddhist; which makes it for me easier to talk with my Indian or Buddhist friends than to even the most intelligent Christian. In India it is taken for granted that people in different degrees of spiritual development necessarily need, or necessarily outgrow, supports of certain kinds. May it not be that it is not some particular form of liturgy, or school of religious art, which time is at this moment sweeping away, but the whole concept of the cult, as such, the whole use of spiritual supports of this kind?

Not, indeed, that the cult-images have never been, and may not still be, inhabited by the gods. An English friend, not even a Protestant, not a believer at all, described to me how, on a visit to Prague, she had seen, in one of the churches there, an old woman praying. Her eyes were fixed in loving adoration upons some baroque Christ; and my friend distinctly saw the lips of the statue move in answer. Another friend—again not a Catholic, though a believer—

136

was given a medal of the Blessed Virgin which had been blessed by a very holy Spanish nun. She was herself at the time in a condition of intense concentration upon a spiritual and emotional problem of her own; and, sitting with the medal and looking at it, she saw, to her astonishment, brownish-red drops running down from the extended hands of the Virgin onto her own fingers which held it. She wiped the drops from her fingers and found that they were blood; and together with this physical manifestation, she seemed to understand some profound meaning of love and suffering. To her the symbol had spoken, the outward form was the vehicle of reality.

Lisa Hill, until her retirement Professor of Russian in Cambridge, described to me how with her own eyes (and, what is more, in America) she had seen a weeping icon of the Virgin, whose tears, as minute as seed-pearls, proportionate to her paper face, ran down ceaselessly, so that the bottom of the cheap print was sodden like blotting-paper. It is all the same whether the weeping figure be of paper or of dream; that which weeps may use any vehicle; for there is a weeper. We are surprised, incredulous, even shocked, when the vehicle of the tears is of paint or paper; but if in a dream the Virgin weeps, we do not doubt the reality of the sorrower. If once the sacramental seemed to inhere in the icons and symbolic enactments of the cult, the power to trans-substantiate to reside in its priests, this is no longer the truth of experience. For me the Church has not been the trans-substantiator; and the sacramental, the trans-substantiate, we can meet only where itself meets us.

I do not know how, unless by that quality itself, we may recognize the holy, the numinous; and in certain dreams and visions (and also when the curtain of nature has been lifted) I have known that presence. Those 'images of wonder' brought forth, in dreams, like the sacred objects carried by the priest celebrating the Orthodox liturgy from behind the icon-painted screen (the Book, the Cup, the bread and the wine) itself an emblem of the gate or barrier between two

137

worlds now open, now closed) and all that comes and goes between, have seemed mysteries for a moment shown, given from the One Mind. No one, as Edwin Muir says, knows the whole Fable; only parts of it. Perhaps the soul is, in its very nature, 'naturally Christian'; but who can set limits to the inexhaustible indwelling Imagination? Of those few I have been shown in dreams most are themselves central symbols of the Christian mysteries: the Tree, holy well, the sign of the Cross, and that sword of light once held in my dreaming hand. May not the withdrawal of the numinosity formerly projected upon the symbolic enactments of the cult to the source itself, within the ever-living imagination within each of us, be a sign not of irreligion but of spiritual maturity? If I spoke only for myself I would hesitate to say this; but the experience is widespread, not among those who do not believe, but among those who do.

Living in this leaf-fall of a civilization (or is it of a world?) I have witnessed with sorrow and with fear the showering down of dead leaves which were once—even within my own memory—informed with life. Not only from churches but from the civil order (insofar as this is an expression of spiritual and intangible values) the life has been progressively withdrawn. In the generation before my own, T. S. Eliot remained within the tradition he would have wished to see continue; he, and David Jones, were perhaps the last poets of that tradition. Yeats saw the darkness approaching, the tide rising; but his hope lay not in any turning or stemming of the tide, but in that which lies beyond civilizations, the God of the gyres, the Indian Brahman whose outbreathings create worlds and whose inbreathings withdraw them from existence. But Yeats too was still among the artificers of Byzantium, the Graeco-Christian civilization, preserved in Ireland beyond its time elsewhere. It is my generation which has seen the end.

I would not have tried so hard to adhere to the Church from personal motives—indeed I have never looked to religion for spiritual support, rather the reverse: if my adherence would help to save the Church, mainstay of civilization, then I would willingly adhere. But if I am to be true to what I imaginatively perceive (for what such intuitions are worth) I must say that it is of no use to try to keep the leaves from falling, green though they once were, and lament as we must their fading. The nihilists would agree; but they desire the death of the tree, the dismantling of civilization, nor do they believe in those divine originals Christendom has embodied and reflected. Yet it is not those leaves which cling longest against the wind of change that are obedient to the tree's life, but the seed cast adrift, the end as it is the beginning of the life-cycle. The great tree is at this time showering down its leaves in a process of death which cannot be arrested, and whose record is everywhere to be read in the nihilism of the arts, of social life, in a thousand images of disintegration, in the reversion of civilized society, it may be, to a state of barbarism.

The mustard-seed (smallest of all seeds), is a symbol of the dimensionless point through which the timeless interior order ('the Kingdom of Heaven is within') issues into the time-process, and returns again into the inner world. From the seed the tree grows; as Rome from the apostolic, Byzantium from a marriage of the Greek and the patriarchal vision. What is latent in the seminal vision is, in the process of time, projected into the thousand arts and *mores* of a civilization; or of an individual life-time. But when the process has been completed, when all that was latent in that seed has been made manifest, is there not then a reversal, an inbreathing, a withdrawal, as the psychologists would put it, of those projections which, reflecting and embodying themselves, were the agents of civilization? The tooth even of a dog glows with holiness when worshipped with devotion; but is the tooth ultimately necessary?

Those who are indissolubly wedded to the external forms, whether of a religion or of a culture, must at this time despair; unable to withdraw from these what for centuries has been projected into them, they lose, when these fail, portions of their souls; but those who are able to rediscover within themselves all that has been progressively withdrawn from our dismantled world, need not fear the withdrawal of the informing presence from the beautiful forms itself created.

The process of death cannot be arrested, civilizations cannot be saved; but there are the seeds, the living among the dead, who do not participate in the collective disintegration, but guard their secret of immortality, the essence of what has been and may be again. Who can say into what soil these seeds may be sown, or into what region of the universe the harvest of the world is gathered?

(And re-reading this manuscript in 1976, I dreamed, last night, the words, repeated again and again, 'Set the axe to the root of the tree'.)

*

A Judgement

HARDEST OF all to write; for here, if at all, I must confess that mortal truth which throughout a lifetime I have sought to evade; or declare that immortal truth which I have looked for. The one as hard as the other; and how related? I do not know. Here I reach only the boundaries of my own ignorance. Every being is finite, can contain only so much of either knowledge; and yet what each is capable of experiencing, of attaining, must suffice. Has my own life sufficed? That, it now seems to me, is the only question which in the end remains. For happiness and suffering alike become, once past, something else altogether.

But since it has been above all poetic truth I have followed, tried to discover always that good, that best Socrates never ceased to speak of, poetic justice it must have been (the only kind I ever acknowledged) that brought me at last to stand my judgement in Greece itself.

I had written thus far when, in 1966, there came a letter from Philip Sherrard, to whom I had shown my work in progress:

'I've been thinking about the last part of your book, and it seems to me that what you have to do is not to say anything at all about the Church or about Traditional doctrine or anything of this kind—you've said all that in your Blake book, and anyhow it's not what is wanted. What is wanted is something absolutely simple and what is the heart of your life and what has been distilled from the experience and the suffering, and this put down in words that are free from jargon, even of the most exalted kind. And I'm sure that what this thing is—what you have found and what you can communicate from within as perhaps few other people can—is connected with, almost born from. . . your relationship with Gavin, and that is the extraordinary insight this has given you into that fantastic mystery which we call love. Love human and love divine—love divino-human—human love moving into eternity, eternity moving into human life through love: isn't that your theme?'—and a page or two on:

'. . . when one thinks of the absolute travesty of love and sex in our age, its vilification and emptiness, its lack of beauty—could there be anything better to do than to try to clean this filthy slate—not from the outside but from the inside? . . . But this living of the central mystery and miracle, that is what I would ask to learn and be initiated into.'

So I decided to go to Greece, there to finish my work in the Sherrards' house, in a bare room with bed, chair and table where I have often worked. I brought the record of my life to place before Philip's judgement; the judgement of a lover of poetry, an Orthodox Christian, more well-read than I am myself in all the literature of the world's wisdom; he would read my record in the light of that perennial truth by which all must finally be judged; which has long been, for Philip as for myself, the only measure; and—I see it now very well—a friend on whose partiality I could rely not to judge me too hardly.

In that room I found in a book some words from Conrad's *The Arrow of Gold*; which seem a better comment than any I might make upon Philip's letter: 'In every, even terrestrial, mystery there is as it were a sacred core. A sustained commentary on love is not fit for every eye. A universal experience is exactly the sort of thing which is most difficult to appraise justly in a particular instance.'

But that perennial wisdom had appointed for me another judge; I had invoked the Judge of whose coming no one knows the day or the hour; and the one consciousness that pierces up and down through every plane of being brought

142

it about that in the appointed hour the judge should appear who was to pronounce that sentence against which we cannot plead.

So perfect is the pattern of destiny that, at the time when it was necessary we should meet, Gavin and I were once more brought together. Nearly seven years had passed; our houses in London had been mere yards apart, in physical distance; I had visited mutual friends in Scotland; yet never once had circumstances brought us together. Since the exchange of letters at the time of his marriage there had been no communication between us; only that one meeting in the street, when we had scarcely paused, he on his way, I on mine. And as our first meeting had come unsought, so now again.

I say unsought; but was this really so? Had I not, all these years, been waiting for Gavin, though only inwardly, not overtly? I had made it a rule, which had become second nature, never to look across Paultons Square towards No. 9; some sense of honour forbade me to do so, as it forbade me to try to learn anything beyond the bare minimum about Gavin or his activities. If he wished me to know, he would tell me; if he wished to seek me out, he would do so. It was through no doing of mine that from the house of Philip Sherrard (who is, after all, one of my oldest and most valued friends) I could look down on the pantile roof of Gavin's brother's house. Sometimes that brother invited me to drink ouzo with him on a terrace looking over the sea to Mount Parnassus between a palm and a cypress whose shapes stood, like the rowan and the waterfall pool at Sandaig, in Gavin's consciousness also. Just as, when I visited Gavin's friends (and through him now my friends) John Lorne Campbell, of Canna, and his wife Margaret Fay Shaw, I returned, above all, to Gavin's horizon, waiting always to catch a glimpse, from the *Loch Arkaig* or the *Western Isles*, of a speck in the distance that was the Sandaig lighthouse.

The day after my own arrival, Gavin came on a visit to his brother; for Gavin, not Philip, was my appointed judge.

143

And the divine justice was to be more terrible than anything I had ever dreamed, because altogether different from
anything I had foreseen.

Heaven knows I did not seek him out; would have avoided
him, had he so wished; but this was not so; perhaps he too
wanted to make peace. He came and stood on the shore
where I was bathing and waited for me. He looked as if he
too had suffered; as if a dark shadow enveloped him. We
talked, all that noon, down under the olives outside the
little *taverna* by the mother-of-pearl sea; for many hours. He
told me, in outline, the story of his life in those intervening
years.

(What folly made me suggest that he should read the
manuscript of my autobiography, which I had with me? I
had not, after all, written it in order to publish it—during the
lifetime of my parents I could not in any case have done
so—but under the compelling necessity to understand, and
by understanding, make somehow bearable, my life. I was
not attempting to justify myself, indeed, but to discover the
truth. And yet how ugly the self-portrait I had drawn, I
had not realized. It is one thing to write such a record;
quite another to read it. I was probably the last person capable of doing that. Why did I feel I must show it to Gavin?
Perhaps I still wanted him, in Helen's word, to 'see'; but was
unable to understand, even now, *what* he would see. I
thought of him still, I suppose, as part of myself; so ac-
customed was I to talking to him in my thought as if he
were there, as if he were the daimon whose image I suppose
some Jungian would say I had projected on him, that I did
not think how painful such a reading might be to him. Helen
Sutherland had read my manuscript, and Philip; but they
saw everything, including myself, from quite another
standpoint.

So he read the book; as far as the curse and the Tree, no
farther. After he had done so we met again; and while the
moon travelled from her rising behind pine-clad Kandile to
throw down for us her unheeded path of light across the

water as she moved from Helicon to Parnassus, from Parnassus towards Pelion, the full bitterness of the truth I had not seen was laid bare; Gavin's truth.

Cecil Collins had read the auguries in my tea-leaves before I left England; 'You are now asked', he said, 'to make a complete sacrifice.' Sacrifice, I then thought, what more have I to lose? It seemed unlikely that my death could be meant, for in this there would be nothing which could be called sacrificial. But he was right; I still had certain memories which I treasured; and I was asked, now, to sacrifice not only the present, but the past as well; to abandon all the places recollection might still have visited; of my days of happiness at Sandaig, nothing was to be left me now, or for the future. I have to live the rest of my life with the retrospective knowledge that in those times and places in which I had been happy because I had thought myself invisibly companioned, I had been alone. Fortunately for my power to survive the intervening years I did not know then what I learned that night; nor do I think I could have believed it, my imagination would not have encompassed it, so near those days whose deep beauty was an experience lived and not a memory only. For Gavin was entirely to disown and to deny any participation in a relationship I had thought mutual; 'outrageous' was the word he used. Canetti had been quite right when he had so solemnly assured me, 'Gavin does not love you, Kathleen.' Not in any sense of the word love; not at any time. Canetti had, it is true, done his utmost to undermine my own love for Gavin: 'You do realize, Kathleen,' he had once said, 'that Gavin *dyes his hair*?' Useless, of course; I only retorted with Yeats's lines about

> '. . . looking for the face I had
> Before the world was made'

Our standards, Canetti's and mine, were, first and last incommensurable.

And yet I had seemed to have my reasons; why had Gavin,

145

then, lent me his house, not once but many times, speaking of it always, as I did also, as of a place we shared? Why, once when we were speaking of death, had Gavin when I had asked him what, if he were dying, he would do, said 'send for you'; why asked his brother to rent me an old and beautiful tower on his estate on whose spiral stone stair the doves laid their eggs undisturbed? These and like memories had long been like fixed stars in my firmament; but now the stars fell from heaven.

'What a long time ago all that seems' he said; to him an episode almost forgotten, to me the forever-written story of my book of life. Yet have not I myself written of my marriage with Charles as something long past, because I had chosen to forget, as Gavin had forgotten me? Is anything ever cancelled from that dread Book of Judgement, and may we not, at death, have to read those pages, made present again before our eyes, which we have thought to blot out by putting them from our minds? Gavin too, though my judge, must himself be judged; though not by me.

He had not loved me; Tambi, who had consigned Gavin to my care (and had I not, at the time, wondered what could be wrong about a situation which brought Gavin to my door through Tambi's introduction?) had at the same time forced me upon Gavin; who had, for his part, never heard of me. 'That woman is very lonely,' he had said, and nagged Gavin to invite me out, and so forth; and he had done so, perhaps because he was under some obligation to Tambi, who was useful to him at the time. Gavin laughed—we both did—when this double plot came to light; so like Tambi; and a good idea, so far as it went. All sorts of things fitted into place—a painter friend of Tambi's who some years before had inexplicably sent me boxes of *soleil d'or* narcissi from the Scilly Isles. Had Tambi long had in mind that I needed a lover? But how dangerous a thing it is to practise such deceptions. Hardy's Farmer Maybold might have lived quietly enough as Bathsheba's neighbour, but for that

146

valentine, which he took to be an overture. When we think our love is welcome, we lay aside our defences. It is not in my nature to make a first advance, even in friendship. That had been my one defence; a defence also, perhaps, for others too, against my too extreme emotions.

And Canetti; had he too deceived me? True he had warned me; but that Gavin had a mistress, even at the time when, first visiting Sandaig, I had thought my place in his life the counterpart of his in mine—that Canetti had not told me. My instinct to fly when I had seen that pair of gloves in Gavin's studio had been right. I asked him, later, whether he had known of this; if, indeed, it was true—for Gavin might only have been trying, after all, to hurt me as much as he could. Yes, Canetti said; he had known, but had carefully—how carefully!—kept it from me; because, he said, I could not have endured to know the truth. Truth again! Canetti's truth this time; the truth of the compassionate man who does not trust God; who builds for us little saving edifices, vital illusions. What folly, what presumption! For they collapse in the end, long before the end. *Magna est veritas et praevalebit*; but only the truth of God. Into what net of lies I had allowed myself to be woven! Gavin told me, that night, of another parallel: to him Canetti had said, 'Kathleen for you is the abyss;' as to me he had said, 'Gavin for you is the abyss.' Canetti denies having said this, and I am willing to believe him, but not to lose the symmetry of the pattern; for if he did not say it, he should have said it, for it proved true. But as to Gavin being for me 'the abyss', I have learned from William Blake to commit myself to the void.

But Gavin himself—what had his motives been? God knows; perhaps he had really set out to be kind to me; perhaps even pitied me? and when I received with tears what for love was too little but for friendship very much, what could he have done? '*Il faut aimer pour savoir qu'on n'est pas aimé. Quand on n'aime plus, on est toujours assez aimé.*' Perhaps he liked me well enough while I, like poor Proust, suffered all the

147

while from not being loved; liked me well enough until he could stand no more of my love, and broke out in irritation; or withdrew himself inwardly as I would have done myself had I ever allowed any one in love with me to get even a foot inside the door of my life. Gavin, it seems, had been kinder, infinitely kinder, than I would have been, in his situation.

Of course Canetti spared me nothing, afterwards; told me all he had then withheld, confirmed what Gavin himself had told me; and so did Sonia Orwell, and so did others. What concerns us we always come to know, in the end; and this is right. What an atrocious deception to keep any human being in a state of ignorance or illusion in matters of vital concern to us! And yet, I could not, then, have believed what even as Gavin spoke the words, there at Katounia, seemed like a dream.

It may seem a strange irony that Philip should, of all things, have written that it is only on the theme of love that he would ask to learn from me. 'If one is in love one can invent many reasons why one's love is unlike anybody else's, both in quality and kind, and this I think you have done somewhat naïvely. You should not forget that your readers will judge you by this account of your life.' That was Gavin's comment, which may stand, for what it is worth, beside Conrad's 'sacred core', which, of course, belongs to every true experience of love, not, certainly, to mine only. I am concerned with values, not with my own case-history. I do not suppose my love to be 'unlike anybody else's', except in detail; but I had hoped, in exploring my own experience, to discover, perhaps, universal things. All poetry makes the same assumption of universality in particulars.

If that vision of perfection Plato and Dante and Shelley saw (beholding in imperfect humanity the image and inprint of eternal beauty) then, yes, I know a little about love. But if by love the spirit that suffereth long and is kind, I know almost nothing. 'Tell me one single person who has

148

been close to you in your life,' Gavin said, 'whom you have not destroyed—your parents, your children, your husband, myself whom you say you loved. What was your love for me but an infatuation? You are a destroyer, Kathleen.' I could not defend myself; for it is so. So little, during those days at Sandaig, did I see myself as a destroyer that I had placed myself under the protection of Milton's lines; and at that time the lines of verse I to myself recited as I walked the hills were from *Samson Agonistes*:

> All is best, though we oft doubt
> What th' unsearchable dispose
> Of highest wisdom brings about,
> And ever best found in the close.
> Oft he seems to hide his face,
> But unexpectedly returns,
> And to his faithful Champion hath in place
> Bore witness gloriously; whence Gaza mourns
> And all that band them to resist
> His uncontroulable intent,
> His servants he with new aquist
> Of true experience from this great event
> With peace and consolation hath dismist,
> And calm of mind, all passion spent.

But all was not best at the close, nor was there peace nor consolation from the event.

Yet I had felt Gavin, often enough, to be my destroyer. I think his judgement was just, and my own mere self-deception; I thought because I suffered that it was he who was making me suffer; whereas it was nobody but myself. Suffering is of all things the most deceptive; for when we are suffering we are unaware of the pain we may ourselves be causing; often by the very fact of the state of suffering we are in.

Beyond the inner circle of those in my life—and Gavin was right about the suffering I had caused my parents and my children—I have, I suppose, done as much good as

149

harm, harm as good; neither more nor less than most human beings; all of which counts for nothing at all before the judgement of the God within. I have, in this record, told my truth, not concealing faults of which I was aware. I had written, even before my fateful encounter with Gavin, that ignorance ignores precisely that of which it is ignorant.

The poets are always blamed, more or less, for the same thing: they are ruthless, or that which drives and possesses them is. Yet that is not how it seems to those who, perceiving immortal beauty, can do no other than follow it and strive to give it expression. 'Looked at from the shadow-side, ideals are not beacons on mountain-peaks, but task-masters and gaolers . . . foisted upon mankind by a clever ruse.' Jung said that. Blake had said much the same, in much better prose, about 'the delights of Genius, which to Angels look like torments and insanity. . . .' I had all these years thought I was holding up before Gavin (in the poetry of the relationship as I saw it no less than in my published work) the reflected images of holy things. I had thought that by holding before him this beauty I could do him every good; and perhaps after all he did glimpse something in that glass.

I had been at first wounded at heart by what seemed a wilful denial of a shared vision; and if afterwards my bewilderment intensified to an anguish in which I invoked the divine avengers it was because I saw all those heavenly and holy treasures profaned as if they had no value, no existence. If to Gavin what to me seemed most real, seemed reality itself, was as if non-existent, was not he the loser?

Laurens van der Post has somewhere told a Bushman fairy-tale of a heavenly milk-maid married by a mortal. She made one condition—that until she gave him leave he should not open a basket she had brought with her from the sky. Of course he did so; and laughed at her because he found it empty. 'Empty?' she asked; then told him that it had in fact been filled with heavenly treasures; but because he did not see them, she was compelled to leave him and

150

return whence she had come. So long ago the world had known the secret of every woman's love. And if he has good right to say that I did not meet his need, I can say the same: had he given me that intangible support I as a poet needed so greatly (Tambi was right there) had he not begun, little by little, to undervalue and misconceive me, I might have done better, and all those years of desolation which were to follow been, instead, fruitful. I believe our relationship should have been what I dreamed it was—a lifelong Platonic love. But—so it was, and the cause of failure lay in ourselves.

Parting, the moon casting our shadows on the spent dust; exhausted by hours of torment given and received, we kissed, at last, as long ago we would have kissed at parting, and Gavin said, 'write *something* kind about me.' And even then I did not realize that I had not, in fact, written anything kind about Gavin; only my own dreams and fantasies.

Comparing the harvest of our lives over those seven years, I could show only a few poems; he, *Ring of Bright Water* and all his later books. And if I had brought on those nearest to me nothing but unhappiness, he, of all those he had taken under his protection, had not lost one; all had been set on their ways by his compassionate understanding and active help. I reminded him how, long ago, he had quoted, as his own deepest belief, Traherne's 'Never was anything in this world loved too much but many things have been loved in a false way: and all in too short a measure.' Now I saw it as possible that the little friendship Gavin had felt for me had been more generous than my much 'love'; for I had not answered his needs, but wound about him the trammels of my emotions. I did not know I was making emotional demands at all; nor is love a 'demand' when it is returned—who calls the love of children 'demanding'? Children take for granted that they will be loved, and what is most terrible is that they should ever not be. Why is it so seemingly impossible for grown men and women to love one another with the same simplicity? It seemed to me, as we sat under the vine and the olive, unable, like two children, to make up our quarrel, that probably we would both have done so, if we could; that both of us knew, at the bottom of our hearts, that we still were, and always would be, as much part of one another's lives as we had always been; but neither of us could say this, things had gone too far, we were too old, too tired really to care enough; like two old animals who go their lonely ways. Or rather, two different things were simultaneously true—all that Gavin had said, all that I had believed; and none of it. Children understand this perfectly; and that too seems to be a capacity lost with age. In fact I said something of the kind to Gavin as we parted: that I had not taken all this so very seriously; and he replied, with what seemed relief, 'I didn't really think you had.' I think it possible that all Gavin's sexual adventures and misadventures, all my wrongs and heroics, are only superficial, are nothing but children's make-believe in comparison with what really was and is and always will be between us. But I may be mistaken.

*

January the fourteenth, 1976. In my three-roomed cottage on the Border, bought with my mother's legacy, and near the places she loved and the places I loved; near Gavin's Solway, where the skeins of geese fly over, in spring and autumn, and the childhood home that he had loved, I conclude my story. The sky is grey and the north-east wind is howling and rumbling, the wild free wind I loved as a child at Bavington; not many miles away. A long way from Cambridge; a sanctuary, though not a paradise.

Am I any nearer to the truth now than on the day Gavin and I so fatefully, indeed so fatally, met? God knows; nor does it matter any more, for Gavin is dead, and what help now can my thoughts be to him? Or are our thoughts, above all, important to the dead? Or have I not, all the time, tried to disguise from myself the real situation, saying that I experienced this or understood that—the plain facts—facts, not dreams—that I lost Mij; and that I laid on Gavin a curse

152

that may have caused his death. He was younger than I; he should have been living now, and how much he would have found still to do, among his wild creatures.

I began to write my story all those years ago because, in my own suffering—for the suffering was real enough though perhaps all self-caused, and in no way an extenuating circumstance—I had to try to understand. Why had I to try to understand? What impells us? We do not make ourselves, we are what causes unknown, rooted in the past, in the universe itself, in the physical earth and in whatever spiritual worlds there may be, have made us. A growing-point, each of us, of the one life, of the 'one consciousness'. What the final purpose is none living knows; only the imperative. I did not write this record in order to publish it, to justify or condemn myself before men and women; nor yet to withhold it. I wrote it because I must and if it can serve any useful purpose to others struggling, as I have struggled, to live a life, why should fear of ridicule or censure hold me back? I am aware that the person who emerges from these pages is as terrible as that demon-face of the Lady Rokujo in the Nō play of *Aoi*. And yet, all my life, how hard I have tried—tried to understand, to discover the good and to live by it, to bear witness, to accomplish something. Not for myself, in particular; but because of that innate imperative. I wish I could say 'for the greater glory of God'; that is what I would have wished to be able to say. Only the word, God, should perhaps be avoided; it has meant too many things to mean anything. But at the end of this story I see how ridiculous such a claim would be. I have been blind and evil; but perhaps the devils also struggle as best they can to do what they must.

Well, Gavin wrote and published his story: *Raven Seek thy Brother*. Of how I had laid on him a curse to which he thereafter attributed all the tragic disasters that befell him. My poor father wanted to sue Gavin and his publishers for libel, little knowing how much truth lay in his story. Longmans, so I was told (it may only be rumour but it could

153

well be true) were a little nervous about libel, but Gavin assured them that they need have no fear. And he was right, of course: right for two reasons—the first, that knowing me he knew that I would never bring a libel suit ever, under any circumstances, against any one, least of all himself; and, more important, that I would not deny the truth of what he had written; even though, for good measure, he had thrown in an added clause to my curse, extending it to his circle of friends and any of these who might visit Sandaig. But even in that invention there may have been a basic truth, that I was perhaps jealous or disapproving of some of these. It might have been so. Nor indeed can I blame Gavin for writing such a book, since he had after all, seen mine.

'Gavin is lucky to be able to blame everything on you,' his brother said to me. There is some truth in that; for he was, after all, very well able to make mistakes on his own account. He made the mistake of marrying; he made the mistake of leaving Sandaig and his otters Edal and Teko in the care of young, and if only for that reason, irresponsible people. He involved himself in various Evelyn Waugh-like adventures in North Africa; many things which he cannot, by any stretch of credibility, lay to my charge. When first I met Gavin he was involved already in one of his periodic crises; and truth to say he was ever at his best when, having got himself into some desperate situation, he set to work not only to extricate himself from it, but to turn it to account. . . This was his temperament; for Gavin, the very idea of security and peace and quiet was unimaginable. That was after all why I—and why through his books so many others —loved him.

But the fire which destroyed the house at Sandaig, and Edal? Was that the result of my terrible invocation, 'Let Gavin suffer here as I am suffering now'? If it is so, then indeed I am guilty. Casting my mind back I remember how once, going down the hill to Sandaig, long before we had so fatally quarrelled, I had thought the house was on fire, and had said so to Mary Macleod, who was with me, and could confirm it if she would. I dare say she holds me responsible for all. Was it some trick of light, or a precognition? Or both? I was greatly alarmed at the time, I remember, being myself then in charge of the house. When I read in the press of the burning of the house at Sandaig it never crossed my mind that I was the cause or that Gavin could have thought me so. I sent him a telegram of sympathy—for had not that house, to me also, been the place most dear on earth? I knew what it must mean to him. And he wrote me in reply and we did then in some measure begin to make up our quarrel. It was not until *Raven Seek thy Brother* was published that I realized that Gavin really did attribute the burning of the house to my curse. And even then—for I was both hurt and angry that after all my only place in any book of Gavin's was not as a friend who had loved and helped him once but as the woman who had laid a curse on him. But if that was how Gavin saw me, it was, if only in that respect, the truth. I never wished him ill; and in those long years of separation there was in my own heart only the ragged pain of separation, the longing to be reconciled. Perhaps he felt that longing dragging at him and interpreted that as ill-will; for, certainly, the sense of another person's unwanted thoughts flowing towards one constantly, could well be felt so. For good or ill we were, after all, attuned. To me Gavin was like a part of myself; he may well have felt something of the kind, however much he might have wished it not to be so.

Yet it had all seemed so different at the time; as if one were to draw a picture blindfold, and then, the bandage removed, see some terrible shape. . . .

Raven Seek thy Brother concludes with an open question: after the fire which destroyed his house and his otter, was the curse spent? In that open question Gavin was to lay his own death to my charge. For nothing, thereafter, went well with him. He bought the little lighthouse isle between Kyle of Loch Alsh and Kylakin, on Skye; but that little rocky islet, with its views of wild cold grandeur to the north, with its eider-colony, its secure enclosure for Teko, was not for

Gavin what Sandaig had been. I visited him there twice; the first time soon after *Raven Seek thy Brother* had been published. It is characteristic of our relationship that there were no recriminations whatsoever on either side. I have said that there was much of our childhood in what we were to one another; and when we behaved like children, who forget the dreadful things they have just done to one another as if nothing had happened, all was well. As adults, nothing went well between us.

Gavin tried to make me stay on, but I did not; he asked me to come back soon; but when I did so we again quarrelled bitterly. Justly proud of the success of the film of his *Ring of Bright Water* he spoke of this, and played me a record of a piece of 'pop' music written to the words; my words, from a poem I had written at Sandaig in happy days. I had waited for some word about the film which might have recognized that I had ever played any part in that story, other than as the cause of Mij's death. But he said no word, not even that he hoped I had not minded too much a film in which my own part was, after all, re-enacted. Or so my friends told me, for my own pain was too great for me to have ventured to see the film. It was only after Gavin's death that I at last forced myself to read *Ring of Bright Water*; though I had carried the book half round the world with me, unread. And after listening to that record—it was very pleasant, I remember—it was not the music as such that hurt me—I had said in bitterness of heart not, indeed, what really made my heart bitter, which was that he had not spoken that word I had waited for, of—not gratitude, but recognition, companionship, even compassion—at all events something that made of me not a stranger—something about the use he had made of my poem which made him think—or pretend he thought—that I was trying in some way to 'cash in' on his fame. Now that of course is, even allowing that Gavin truly saw the shadow-side of me that my friends were not aware of—the devouring female spider of emotional possessiveness—unthinkable. I have never in my life done

156

anything for money, and from Gavin that was the last form of restitution I wanted—but I was too proud to say, what I hoped he might have understood, that his *Ring of Bright Water*, that was to become a film, and then a legend, because it was written in his heart's blood, was written in my heart's blood also.

And yet, why could I not see that to Gavin Mij's death must have cancelled any former debt of love between us? Yet I could not bring myself to face this, or to realize that in assigning to me only the part of the woman who had laid on him a curse, I was assigned my due. Why did I continue to hark back to a paradise I had myself destroyed?

So real that paradise had been that I still could not believe that the end of the story had been the end; and I still went on hoping that I could still have the place in his life that I had thought was mine, the participation, the shared experience from which *Ring of Bright Water* had been written. Perhaps a murderer feels so—hoping still for the love of the wife or lover he has killed (why do I say 'he' when it is 'she' —myself—I mean?); and goes on acting as if it had not happened, not from the desire of deceiving others but because unable to believe what has been done in an instant has undone the reality of a lifetime. So Gavin supposed that I—who had, so long ago, lent him, or fancied I lent him, the support of my poor little reputation in 'the literary world'— was trying in some way to exploit his fame! Among the many bitter things we said to one another, I remember I exclaimed—unforgivably—'*My* work will be remembered when yours is forgotten.' That was the eye of the tornado; for he always did value my poetry; my books were all, even then, laid on his table. 'That,' he said, 'may very well be true.'

I do not think it is. I believe his *Ring of Bright Water* will live on. I believe also that some poems of mine will live on. I also believe that if I had suffered less in and through my disastrous relationship with Gavin, I would have achieved more. But that is doubtless my fault, not his.

157

I was, on that occasion, beside myself with misery; it was like a nightmare in which we are unable to move or act.

We seemed fatally at cross-purposes, as if we were playing our parts from two different plays. As indeed in some ways we were. And yet, in our poetry how close our roots. Those things we both loved—the hills and the wild places of our childhood, and the earthly paradise we had shared, and destroyed. These things were, for both of us, not only, I believe, our common ground but our deepest reality.

What I had hoped, on that worst of all days, was some word of recognition that I had played in his life and his work some part other than that he assigned to me in *Raven Seek thy Brother*; which to me seemed, against all the evidence, unbelievable. I had wanted him, as Helen understood—as I think any woman would have understood—to *see*; or perhaps simply to understand how much I was suffering and to stop hurting me: it was as simple as that. But many a murderer has perhaps felt just as I did.

I even wondered—or rather some of my friends did—if in *Raven Seek thy Brother* Gavin had not exploited the theme of the curse laid on him because it made a good story. But I do not think, now, that this was altogether so. He had, in the early days, an almost superstitious faith in my power to help him; and I too had believed with my whole being that I could do so. And that one-pointedness of thought is, after all, the secret of the power of all magic. At least I had tried to do so, and he had drawn strength from the faith I had had in him and in my own power. So what more natural than that the dark face of that power should have turned me into a witch in his eyes? And in reality? Of all criminals it is with murderers that I feel most akin, in the terrible realization of how easily a crime of passion can be committed; perhaps I did after all commit just that crime. There are many murders besides those committed with arsenic or pistol.

At one moment, during those intervening years, I did receive a glimpse, which astonished me, of the dread in

158

which Gavin held me. Indeed I could neither understand nor credit what I heard; which I see now as unbelievable obtuseness on my part. Gavin had a friend who happened also to be a close friend of friends of mine; and when he married a young wife, Gavin had given her, to hold during her labour when she was expecting her first baby, a little wooden 'dolphin', a little knot of driftwood from Sandaig shore, that he had formerly given to me, but which I had returned to him. He had told her that 'others besides himself' had made it a potent magical object; and that reported phrase had brought me, in my banishment, a gleam of joy; because I thought I discerned in it some lingering affection and recognition that I had been something more to Gavin than the destroyer of his life. So I had said to my friend, 'Do ask X.. to give it back to me instead of to Gavin, for it was mine once and I would so dearly love to have it again.' Thinking, I suppose, that I would find God knows what comfort in the little piece of wood that for years had lived in my pocket. Certainly I had no harm to Gavin in my thought; for what had made me a little happy was what I took to be a sort of assurance of continuance of affection. When later I was told that when Gavin had heard of my request he had turned pale and had to sit down and recover, I laughed at the story, it seemed so improbable; he had thought I intended to use the dolphin as a charm to work him some ill. It seemed incredible. Yet now I am not so sure; I think he must really have been afraid of me. In the end the dolphin was lost; neither Gavin nor I ever saw it again.

Gavin was already ill, on that last visit, though he did not then know how seriously, for the doctors who had examined him had said there was nothing serious amiss. He suffered from headaches, especially on one side of his head. And one last time I tried to bring him magic help; though not my own magic.

Long ago when Mijbil had been a cub, and was living, still, in Gavin's London studio, some injury to his back had seemed to threaten his life; his hind quarters seemed to be paralysed; and the expert at the Zoo had given little hope and no help. Gavin was in despair; and I bethought me, as a last resort (for at worst it could do no harm) of a certain Brigadier Firebrace, whom I had met with my friends Rupert and Helen Gleadow, who were always much interested in occult matters. This Brigadier had spoken, that evening, of the healing sometimes effected by so-called 'radionics'. This distant treatment presumed non-physical 'radiations' which could be brought to play on some distant patient, if on the 'box' there was a specimen (blood, or spittle or hair or the like) by whose means the healing ray could be 'attuned'. So in our desperation I had taken a small piece of Mij's fur and sent it to Brigadier Firebrace. Mij, on the 'box', made a perfect recovery. Coincidence? I wonder. Gavin had friends, too, whose experience had been similar. There could be, with animals, at least no question of 'suggestion'; and Gavin's friends had well-authenticated evidence of race-horses having been cured in this way. Gavin at the time did not think it was coincidence and neither did I.

When I had left Sandaig for the last time, it had been Edal whose life was despaired of; she was suffering from toothache, and Gavin had taken her to Inverness, to the most skilful vet to be found; who had been quite unable to do anything for her, so strongly rooted are an otter's teeth; and again he was in despair. He scarcely heeded me when I begged, again, for a piece of fur; but finally I was given what I asked for; and sent the fur to the 'box'; but, this time, with my own most passionate prayer for her recovery. Only let Edal recover, I had prayed, and I will never hope to see Gavin again. Edal, against all Gavin's expectation, recovered. Again coincidence perhaps. That time he certainly never gave the matter another thought. This time I begged Gavin to give me a drop of his own blood for the same purpose. Again, it could do no harm, and might help. Is it not foolish to refuse to try everything, even if we do not understand the laws that operate on levels other than the physical? If there are no such laws the worst that can happen is nothing at all. But this time it was of no use.

We made up our last furious quarrel, before I departed. And Gavin asked me to look, on my way to Inverness, into a certain tree-trunk to see if there were young jack-daws in it. There were. I telephoned him that evening from the house of the friend (Gavin's friend) where he had arranged that I should stay; and I heard his beautiful voice, then, for the last time.

Soon after that visit Gavin wrote to me that he had been re-examined and that he was suffering from inoperable, incurable cancer. There was absolutely no hope; he might live for a year, perhaps, and intended, before that time, to come to London. 'I am writing to ask you to accompany me in spirit,' he said. And, God forgive me, in the grief of his dying, I could yet find comfort in those words that surely were, in some sense, more real than all the superficial storms there had been between us, words of love.

I never saw Gavin again; death came mercifully soon. I was in Dublin when I received the telegram. But I knew before I heard. Over my head, on the evening of the day he died, a V-shaped flight of curlew had flown low, reminding me of Gavin's beloved grey-lag geese. I have a photograph given me by him years ago of such a flight, taken as they flew over the Solway. Long ago, in the first weeks of our meeting, we had read together Yeats's *Wild Swans at Coole*; and for those birds that, like his own Solway grey-lags

> . . . lover by lover
> They paddle in the cold,
> Companionable streams

I had seen tears gather in Gavin's blue eyes. In the first poems I ever wrote for him there had been the image of migrant birds, homing to this earth. And as that formation of curlew flew low over me, I had thought, 'Gavin!'. That was a message he would have known I would understand.

Among what rushes will they build,
By what lake's edge or pool
Delight men's eyes when I awake some day
To find they have flown away?

So I took an aeroplane from Dublin to Glasgow, and
travelled on and on, towards Mallaig, and to Canna House,
where Margaret and John Campbell took me in and comforted me as best they could. Gavin had been their friend
too; to him I owed their friendship. Even too much so—
they were ever inclined to believe too well of me, too ill of
him.

His ashes were to be buried at Sandaig where the house
had stood. Bruce Watt, of the *Western Isles*, who had long ago
been one of Gavin's crew on the *Sea Leopard* in the days of
Soay and the shark-fishing, took me to Sandaig; we landed
there, as so often, in the past, with Mij. I was glad to have
Bruce standing beside me; for when the party arrived with
Gavin's ashes and I spoke to Mary Macleod, once my friend,
as I had thought, she was cold and distant; believing doubtless that I was the witch who had caused his death. And that,
too, was a realization that came to me slowly: that to
Gavin's friends I could only seem so. And perhaps they are
right. I laid in his grave a bunch of rowan-berries from the
Tree.

He left me his Order of the Garter tie-pin, which he
always wore, and that had been his grandfather's. He left
very few personal bequests; not even to his brother; perhaps
because death came sooner than he foresaw. So that I do
take comfort from his having, after all, at the end, thought
of me as a friend; with love? affection? compassion? Or
simply as, for better and for worse, 'the woman in his life'?

Three years ago this month I was on Canna for the New
Year, and set out on a stormy morning to cross to Mallaig
on the *Western Isles*. I was the only passenger, and Bruce
called me into his cabin. Presently the weather calmed, and
he gave me the wheel; I guided the boat from Rhum to

162

Eigg, and, leaving Eigg, he said, 'Just hold her towards Sgriol;' and so I steered the *Western Isles* holding her prow towards the mountain above Sandaig, where one midsummer eve Mary and I had seen the fairy-gold of the globe flowers. Bruce talked of his cruises to St. Kilda; of Hugh Miller's *Old Red Sandstone*, and the geological formation of the isles. He did not mention 'the Major'; Western Highland courtesy is perfect. And neither did I, because it would have been too painful to speak his name. But Bruce's arm, very gently and lightly, was laid round my waist. I understood very well what he wished to communicate but could not say.